FINGERBOARD HARMONY FOR

by Gar...

Introduction 2
   How to Use This Book 2
About the Author 3
Intervals 4
   Interval Facts 5
Triads 6
   Second Finger Position 7
   Inversions 7
Seventh Chords 8
The Linear Approach 9
Passing Tones 13
Chord Tones Instead of Roots 14
The Minor Thirds Rule 17
Eighth Notes 18
Extensions 21
Review 25
Hand Positions 27

Second Finger Position 28
Fourth Finger Position 33
The Connection 33
Choosing a Key Center 39
Finding More than One Key 41
The "Three" Chord 43
The "Four" Chord 44
Minor 47
The "Two" Chord 49
The "Five" Chord 49
Shifting 55
Memorizing 58
Secondary Dominants 60
Three/Four 63
Other Chords 68
Putting It All Together 69

PLAYBACK+
Speed • Pitch • Balance • Loop

To access audio visit:
www.halleonard.com/mylibrary

Enter Code
1160-9055-8743-0545

Special thanks to Mitch Sams, John Flitcraft and David Tyree for their help in the development of this book.

ISBN 978-0-7935-6043-1

Visit Hal Leonard Online at
www.halleonard.com

World headquarters, contact:
Hal Leonard
7777 West Bluemound Road
Milwaukee, WI 53213
Email: info@halleonard.com

In Europe, contact:
Hal Leonard Europe Limited
1 Red Place
London, W1K 6PL
Email: info@halleonardeurope.com

In Australia, contact:
Hal Leonard Australia Pty. Ltd.
4 Lentara Court
Cheltenham, Victoria, 3192 Australia
Email: info@halleonard.com.au

Introduction

In high school I was always awful at math (I still am), but when the semester on geometry came around, I got straight As. Fortunately, for me, the bass fingerboard is a very consistently geometric instrument. From day one I've always associated any sound on the bass with its corresponding shape. For instance, a major third is a string and a fret away. That shape (the diagonal line drawn between the two notes on the fingerboard) will result in a major third from any other note on the neck (as long as you've got a string and a fret left to recreate it). By contrast, a major third on a keyboard can be two white notes, two black notes, a white note then a black note, or a black note then a white note. The fingering combinations (shapes) required to play major thirds on any woodwind instrument are even more varied. My approach to fingerboard harmony has always been based on these symmetric shapes.

There are two ways to create harmony on the bass. One way is to play chords. The design and tuning of the bass makes playing and studying chords a fairly inefficient process, even on a 6-string. The other way to create harmony on the bass is to play a series of notes (a line) that reinforce or compliment the sound of the chord. In just about every style of music you're going to need to create a line at some point. Hopefully, this book will give you a consistent way of looking at harmony on the neck so you can play these lines freely.

How to Use This Book

The exercises and examples in this book are cumulative. Each idea or concept is based on the previous exercise and example. I wouldn't recommend skipping too far ahead without making sure you can confidently perform all the previous exercises. It's a very "hands-on" approach. While the exercises may seem easy to understand, be honest with yourself and make sure you can execute them with ease before you're tempted to move on. As with any new concept, it may take a while before this way of looking at harmony becomes "subconscious." At first, be very deliberate and "hyper-conscious" take the time to make sure both your hands and mind understand what's going on with each exercise. Eventually you'll be able to visualize harmony clearly anywhere on the neck.

About the Author

After more than a decade of co-leading Tribal Tech with guitarist Scott Henderson, and their eight CDs, Gary Willis has launched his solo career with the September 1996 release of *No Sweat.* He's performed with Wayne Shorter, Allan Holdsworth, Hubert Laws, Joe Diorio, Robben Ford, and Wayne Johnson. A Texas native, Willis studied composition and improvisation at North Texas State University. After moving to Los Angeles in '82 he became a course leader at Musicians Institute in Hollywood and later taught at California Institute of the Arts in Valencia, California. Since Willis' move to Colorado in 1993, Warner Publications has released *Bass Lessons with the Greats* which includes his chapter on improvisation. Willis' 1991 instructional video is titled *Progressive Bassics.* In addition to this fingerboard harmony book, Hal Leonard will release his composition/solo book in early '97. Two of his compositions are included in Sher Music's *The New Real Book Volume Two,* as well as a solo in *Concepts of Bass Soloing.* He currently lives, writes, teaches, and mountain bikes (not necessarily in that order) with his wife Pamela and their two labrador retrievers, Buster and Jose, in Colorado Springs, Colorado.

Intervals

To begin with, let's make sure we understand a few general music terms. An *interval* is the distance between two notes. The basic intervals come from the major scale.

 Here's a G major scale:

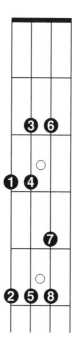

The beginning note in a scale is called the *root*. Each interval based on the major scale is measured from the root and numbered second, third, fourth, etc. When you get to eight it is called an *octave* instead of eighth.

Listen to each interval. The intervals (distances) from the root are as follows:

DISTANCE	NAME	ABBREVIATION
from ❶ to ❷	major 2nd	M2
from ❶ to ❸	major 3rd	M3
from ❶ to ❹	perfect 4th	P4
from ❶ to ❺	perfect 5th	P5
from ❶ to ❻	major 6th	M6
from ❶ to ❼	major 7th	M7

Interval Facts

- The intervals from the root to the second, third, sixth and seventh are called *major* (from the major scale).

- The intervals to the fourth, fifth and eighth are called *perfect.*

- Another name for a major second is a *whole step*.

- On the bass a whole step is two frets, and a *half-step* is one fret.

2 Here's what every interval in an octave sounds like:

NAME	ABBREVIATION
minor 2nd (half step)	m2
major 2nd (whole step)	M2
minor 3rd	m3
major 3rd	M3
perfect 4th	P4
augmented 4th (diminished 5th)	+4, aug4 (-5, dim5)
perfect 5th	P5
augmented 5th (minor 6th)	+5, aug5 (m6)
major 6th	M6
minor 7th	m7
major 7th	M7
perfect octave	P8

It is very important to be able to create these intervals on the bass (as well as identify them when you hear them). All harmony is built on an understanding of these intervals.

Triads

When you play every other note in a major scale simultaneously you get a *chord*. When you play just three of these notes together you get a *triad*.

 Here are the triads created from the G major scale:

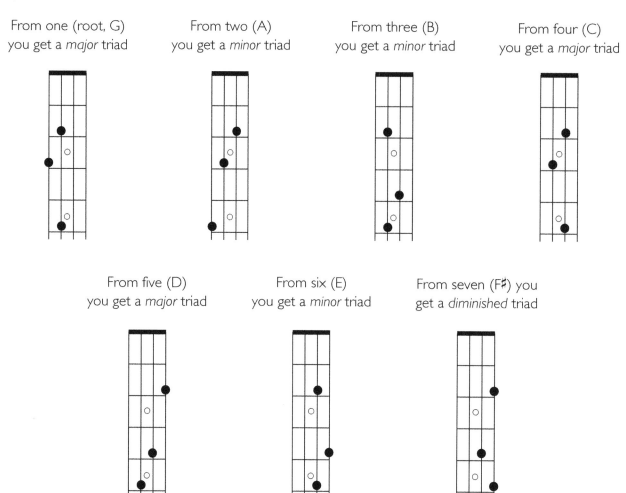

From one (root, G) you get a *major* triad

From two (A) you get a *minor* triad

From three (B) you get a *minor* triad

From four (C) you get a *major* triad

From five (D) you get a *major* triad

From six (E) you get a *minor* triad

From seven (F♯) you get a *diminished* triad

Triad Facts

- Each note in the scale can become the root of a triad. Each root has its own third and fifth to complete the triad.

- Except for number seven, (F♯ diminished triad, key of G) triads 1-6 can be identified by the sound of the first interval (the third).

- Triads built on one, four, and five are major.

- Triads built on two, three, and six are minor.

Second Finger Position

By starting with your second finger on G on the E string you can organize all the triads in the key of G in one location under you hand. This is called a *second finger position.* You may have noticed in this position some notes of the triads have octaves that can also be used to create the same sound. For instance, you can play the triad built off the 7th here:

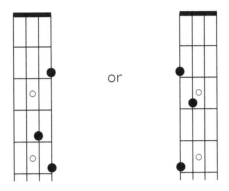

Play all the notes of each triad available in this position (include the octaves of each note).

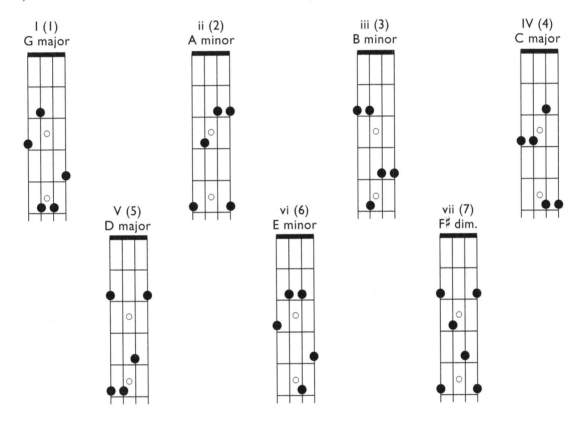

Using only the E, A, and D strings, play through triads 1–7.

Now use only the A, D, and G strings and play 1–7.

Inversions

- When you start a triad with the third or the fifth of a triad you've created an *inversion.*

- A triad started with the third is called *first inversion.*

- A triad started with the fifth is called *second inversion.*

To help you see the inversions, play triads 1–7 in first inversion using all strings. Then play triads 1–7 in second inversion.

Seventh Chords

Two consecutive thirds from a scale create a triad. Three consecutive thirds give you a *seventh chord.*

4 Here are the names and abbreviations of the seventh chords created from each note in the G major scale.

SEVENTH CHORD LOCATION	NAME	TYPE
built from the root	the "one chord"	maj7
built from the 2nd	the "two chord"	m7
built from the 3rd	the "three chord"	m7
built from the 4th	the "four chord"	maj7
built from the 5th	the "five chord"	7
built from the 6th	the "six chord"	m7
built from the 7th	the "seven chord"	m7♭5

The labels for the seventh chords are similar to the ones for triads except for the chords built on the fifth and seventh. Here are the chord tones that each name implies:

- Major 7th: root, major 3rd, perfect 5th, major 7th   ➡   maj7

- Minor 7th: root, minor 3rd, perfect 5th, minor 7th   ➡   m7

- Dominant 7th: root, major 3rd, perfect 5th, minor 7th   ➡   7

- Minor 7(♭5): root, minor 3rd, diminished 5th, minor 7th   ➡   m7(♭5)

The first three of these 7th chords (major 7th, minor 7th, and dominant 7th) constitute the majority of the harmony that we'll be studying for the rest of this book.

The Linear Approach

Guitarists and keyboardists are able to learn harmony on their instruments in a vertical fashion. They are uniformly required to play chords (several notes at a time). This approach to harmony on the bass guitar neck takes into account the role of the bass in almost all situations. Bass players are seldom asked to play more than one note at a time. This means that a different horizontal approach to learning harmony is necessary. Instead of playing all the notes of a particular chord at once, a bassist must imply the sound of a chord one note at a time in a horizontal or linear fashion. In almost every style of music you are required at some point to play a line. Sometimes it's in the middle of a groove or a fill, sometimes it's walking through a tune, and when you're soloing, it's almost completely linear. Creating these lines means making an informed decision about which note gets played on which beat. Just settling for the correct scale or arpeggio rarely gets the job done. The end result can sound fairly academic.

5 Listen to how the C major scale works with Cmaj7.

6 The next example shows what happens when you don't start with the root of the chord.

Scales work only when you begin with the root and ascend. Arpeggios work a little better, but both approaches result in lines that are neither connected or very smooth.

The first thing to understand about the construction of lines is there are strong beats and weak beats that the ear considers before it is satisfied that the harmony is successfully being played.

7 Let's see how the strong beats work. Try playing some random notes along with the audio. Track 7 will have a pair of two-bar Cm7 examples. In the first one you'll hear chord tones of Cm7 (C, E♭, and G) on the strong beats 1 and 3. Play any note you want on the weak beats 2 and 4. In the second two-bar example you'll hear those same chord tones on 2 and 4. Play any note you want on the strong beats 1 and 3. You should notice that no matter what you play in the first two bars you can still get a sense of the Cm7 sound while the second two bars sound much less like Cm7.

The important thing to remember is that with a quarter note pulse the ear needs to hear harmony notes on 1 and 3 and it puts a lot less emphasis on what's played on 2 and 4. The further we get into this process the more we'll effectively learn to use the notes on beats 2 and 4 to reinforce what the ear hears on 1 and 3.

The kind of chords we'll initially be studying are seventh chords in a major key. There are four qualities of seventh chords in a major key:

- major seven (maj7)   minor seven (m7)
- dominant seven (7)   half-diminished seven (Ø7 or minor seven flat five: m7♭5)

To study major diatonic harmony we only need to study the first three (maj7, m7, 7). The half diminished (m7♭5) is almost always found a minor key. We'll get to minor keys later on.

In order to organize a line correctly, we need to know the location of these chord tones on the neck. The notes of any chord on the neck are actually quite close together. Since seventh chords are built in thirds, the largest distance from one note of a chord to the next is a major third. Once you get to the seventh, you're only a half step or a whole step from the next root. In fact, the largest distance you can get from any adjacent chord tone is a whole step.

In the fingerboard diagram below, randomly imagine any pitch that comes to mind and its location on the neck (for instance: F♯, A string, ninth fret). Check on the diagram for its distance to the nearest chord tone. If it's not already a chord tone, you'll find that it's no greater than a whole step from a chord tone.

Cmaj7 arpeggios

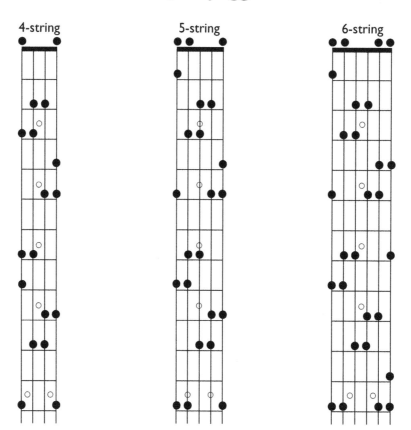

4-string   5-string   6-string

By using chord tones on beats 1 and 3, their proximity on the fingerboard allows us to reinforce the harmony with lines that are made up of only half steps and whole steps. This half-step/whole-step process prevents the common symptom of "jumping around" that creeps into everyone's lines at first and also helps to keep lines from strictly sounding like "scales and arpeggios."

Most of the exercises in this book involve quarter notes and eighth notes. The reason for using quarter and eighth notes is that we're not studying rhythm. The way to avoid studying rhythm is to make the duration of all the notes the same. Once you're comfortable with this process, you'll be able to apply it to anything from half notes to sixteenths.

The best way to learn about the available note choices is to isolate each chord in the area of the neck that we're working on. We'll begin the next few exercises by isolating each chord in the first five frets.

Cm7-F7

To help you memorize the shape of each chord in this part of the neck, use one of the patterns given here for your 4-, 5-, or 6-string bass.

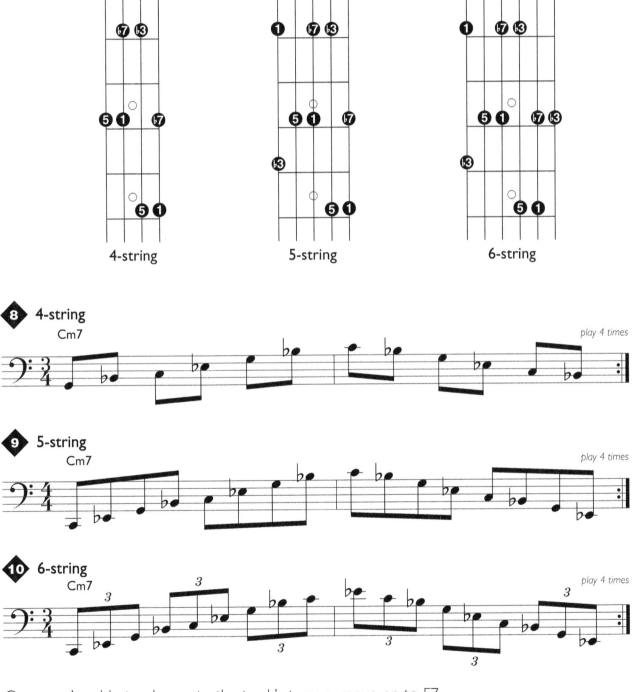

Once you're able to play up to the track's tempo, move on to F7.

F7

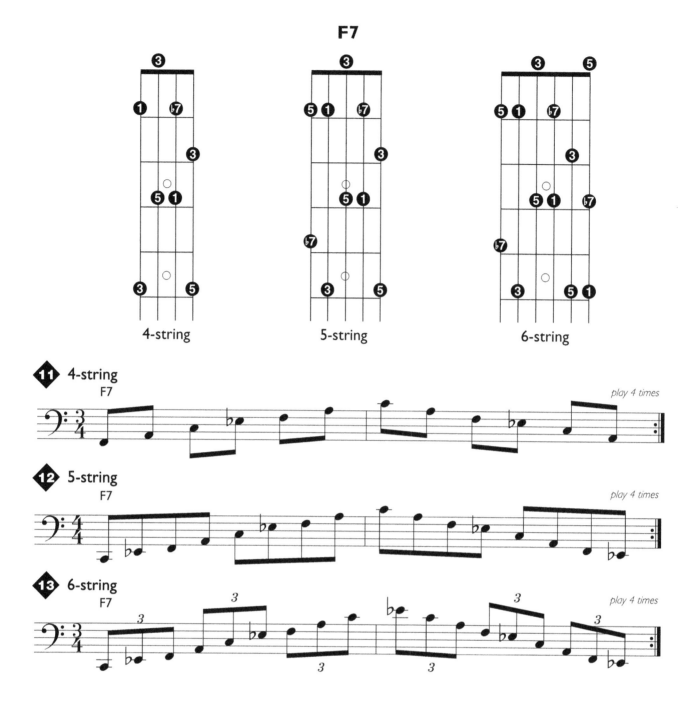

4-string   5-string   6-string

11 4-string
F7

play 4 times

12 5-string
F7

play 4 times

13 6-string
F7

play 4 times

Here's a pattern that combines Cm7 and F7.

14 4-string
Cm7   F7

play 4 times

15 5-string
Cm7   F7

play 4 times

16 6-string
Cm7   F7

play 4 times

As soon as you're comfortable with these patterns, you're ready for the first exercise. Play four notes of Cm7 then four notes from F7. As soon as the chord changes, play the nearest chord tone of the next chord in the direction you're going. Keep your line moving in the same direction until you run out of room (first five frets). If this exercise gives you trouble refer to the previous patterns. As the chords change, the neck should have a different "look." Listen to the track for a sample of the first four measures.

...continue Cm7-F7

As you start to get comfortable with this exercise you can see how important it is to be able to visualize all the available chord tones across the neck.

Passing Tones

A *passing tone* is a note played on a weak beat (2 or 4) that is a whole step or less from the notes before and after it.

We'll be using a passing note only on beat 4 for now. The chords are the same (Cm7 and F7). Begin each measure playing three consecutive chord tones. Use a passing note on beat 4. Keep your line in the same direction until you run out of room (still only using the first five frets). Use the passing note to connect the chord tone on beat 3 to the nearest chord tone of the next chord on beat 1 of the next measure.

...continue Cm7-F7

This example "loops" on a 4-string bass after four measures. In order to benefit from this exercise, begin each four-bar loop with each chord tone available for Cm7 in the first five frets (on a 4-string there are seven available). You can see from this exercise that passing notes can come from the scale, the chord, or sometimes they're chromatic. With the addition of a passing tone you can hear the lines are getting smoother.

Now add a passing note on beat 2. Beats 1 and 3 will be chord tones and 2 and 4 will be passing notes. Don't worry about the direction in this one. Again, a sample line is given as the first four measures on the audio.

...continue Cm7-F7

If you find yourself getting in trouble it's usually caused by wasting a good chord tone on a weak beat.

The first measure doesn't connect as a line because the F on beat 4 is wasted and two Fs in a row are played. Also, the D on beat 3 of the second measure is a thirteenth. The seventh (Eb) is wasted on a weak beat. The second measure sounds O.K. but we're going to save working on ninths, elevenths, and thirteenths (chord tones from above the octave) for later.

An E on beat 4 will allow the line to continue smoothly to F on beat 1. An E on beat 2 of the second measure allows the seventh (Eb) to be played on the strong beat.

Chord Tones Instead of Roots

Another thing you've probably discovered is that playing the root on beat 1 of every measure severely limits your possibilities.

Using chord tones other than the root opens up the possibilities.

...continue Cm7-F7

Stay with this exercise until you can comfortably start on any chord tone of Cm7 and play it in any direction within the first five frets. Visualizing the "pattern" or "grid" of chord tones across the fingerboard allows you immediate access to the notes that reinforce the sound. Also, this exercise allows you to start hearing the chord tones as starting notes of a line instead of the root. In the next exercise we'll avoid starting with the root altogether.

Em7-A7

Use one of the patterns given to memorize the shape of each chord for that part of the neck.

Em7

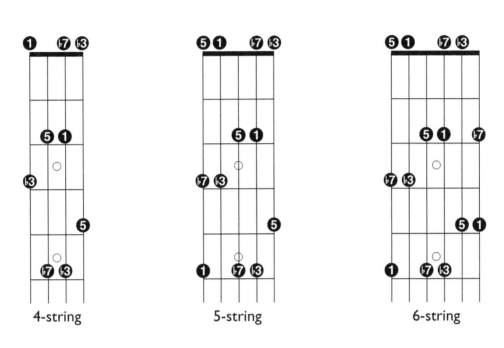

4-string   5-string   6-string

21 4-string
Em7   *play 4 times*

22 5-string
Em7   *play 4 times*

23 *6-string
Em7   *play 4 times*

*The E on the C-string is omitted so the pattern will loop.

Once you're able to play up to the track's tempo, move on to A7.

A7

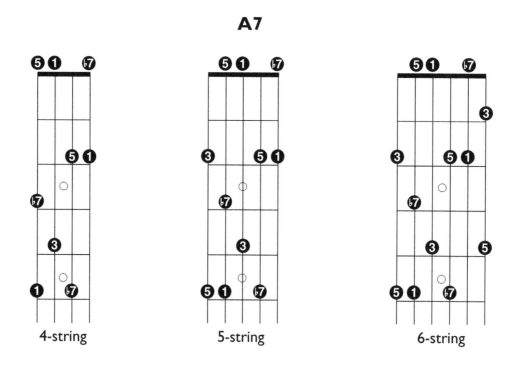

4-string   5-string   6-string

24 4-string

A7   *play 4 times*

25 *5-string

A7   *play 4 times*

*The C♯ on the G-string is added so the pattern will loop.

26 6-string

A7   *play 4 times*

Now use the pattern for your bass that combines Em7 and A7.

In order to avoid the root on beat 1 of every measure you have to be able to change directions. Use chord tones on 1 and 3 and passing notes on 2 and 4 (no roots on 1). Feel free to change directions but make sure your lines extend to the highest and lowest notes available in the first five frets.

...continue Em7-A7

The Minor Thirds Rule

When a line is limited to half or whole steps the decision of which note to use for a passing note is easy. There is usually only one note that will get the correct result.

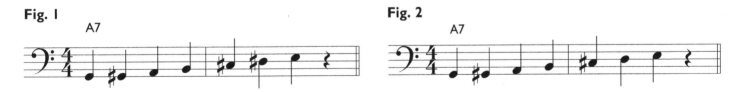

In the first measure, the distance from beat 1 to beat 3 is a whole step (G to A). The only possible note to use on beat 2 is G♯. From beat 3 to beat 1 is a major third (A to C♯). The only possible note to use here on beat 4 is B.

In the second measure from beat 1 to beat 3 the distance between strong beats is a minor third (C♯ to E). There are two choices here that will give you a half-step or whole-step passing tone (D♯ in Fig. 1, or D in Fig. 2). Only one of these will sound good. In this instance the key center will give you the right note. Em7 and A7 are in the key of D major. Therefore, the correct note is D (Fig. 2).

For now, the key centers for each exercise will be given. Later on when we study hand positions we'll work on choosing key centers from a group of chords. Remember, when there is a minor third between chord tones, use a passing note from the key center.

Eighth Notes

One of the benefits of learning to avoid roots in lines involves soloing and the register of the bass. Because of the low register of the instrument it is difficult for a bass solo to sound like it's "above" the harmony, especially if there are a lot of roots in the solo. If the rules of the last assignment are applied to eighth notes with the strong beats coinciding with the quarter note attack and the weak beats on the second of every pair of eighth notes, a very competent sounding solo line will result. The line below shows what the previous Em7-A7 bass line sounds like as eighth notes.

As you play a solo in this fashion, you'll discover the need to change direction often to avoid the root. However, this keeps the line from sounding smooth. In the next exercise we'll go back to using all four chord tones and concentrate on keeping the direction of the line constant.

Dm7-G7

Once again, to get a visual "grid" of chord tones across the neck, we'll begin with the patterns for Dm7 and G7.

Dm7

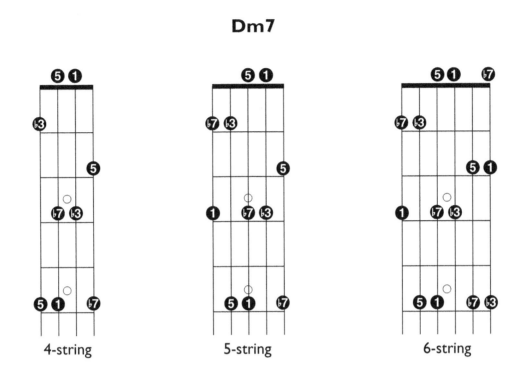

4-string   5-string   6-string

G7

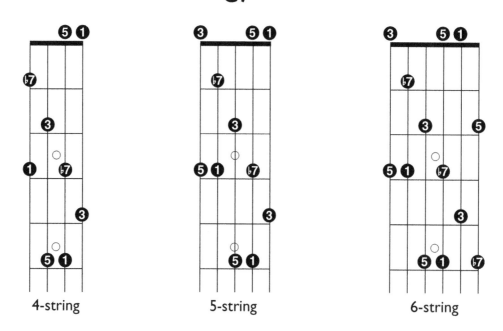

4-string   5-string   6-string

35 4-string
G7   *play 4 times*

36 5-string
G7   *play 4 times*

37 6-string
G7   *play 4 times*

Here's a pattern that combines Dm7 and G7.

38 4-string
Dm7   G7   *play 4 times*

39 5-string
Dm7   G7   *play 4 times*

40 6-string
Dm7   G7   *play 4 times*

The next exercise uses passing tones on beats 2 and 4 and all four chord tones. Dm7 and G7 are in the key of C. Remember to get your passing notes from the key of C when you have a choice. Start with a chord tone on your lowest string (E or B string) and keep the line ascending until you run out of room on your highest string (G or C string, first five frets). Then change direction and descend until you run out of room. Continue ascending or descending until the outer strings are used.

continue Dm7-G7

In the third measure of the next example, you can see the direction has to be interrupted since a passing note is not possible between C and B.

Extensions

Playing lines that maintain direction (whether walking or soloing) results in a more focused musical effect. The listener's interest is held longer because the "idea" of ascending or descending is sustained over a longer period of time. Maintaining direction becomes especially valuable when the chords last for several measures at a time. Eventually the sound of 1, 3, 5, and 7, even though it's been specifically required, becomes limiting and predictable. In the course of creating these lines you've probably stumbled onto some notes that sound good to your ear, but do not fit into the 1, 3, 5, 7 chord tones we've been working on. If you con-tinue spelling chords in thirds past 1, 3, 5, and 7, you get the chord tones 9, 11, and 13. These chord tones are called *extensions*.

42 Let's check out how these extensions sound against a Cmaj7 chord on the track. Play the ninth (D) anywhere on your bass. Now play the eleventh (F) and the thirteenth (A). You should recognize that the ninth and thirteenth sound O.K., but the eleventh doesn't work at all.

Now try these extensions against a dominant 7th chord (track **42** con't). Try the ninth, eleventh, and thirteenth just like before. Just like Cmaj7, the ninth and thirteenth sound good but the eleventh doesn't.

Next is a Cm7 chord (track **42** con't). Try the ninth, eleventh and thirteenth again but this time try a flatted thirteenth (Ab) as well. You should hear different results this time. The ninth and eleventh sound best while the thirteenths don't work quite as well. The natural thirteenth sounds better that the flatted one but is still the worst of the three extensions.

In each of these seventh chords (maj7, m7, and dom7), two out of the three extensions can be used on strong beats of a line:

- For *maj7*, the extensions *nine* and *thirteen* work.
- For *dom7*, the extensions *nine* and *thirteen* also work.
- For *m7*, the extensions *nine* and *eleven* work.

If you rearrange chord tones 1-13, you get the seven notes of a scale:

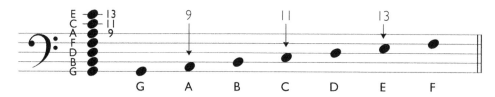

An easier way to remember extensions is that for every scale a seventh chord implies, there is only one wrong note:

For *maj7* and *dom7*, the *eleven* is the weakest extension choice.
For *m7*, the *thirteenth* is the weakest extension choice.

Am7-D7-Gmaj7

Let's take a look at the chord tones for each chord. The extensions are colored gray. There isn't a convenient way to create a pattern combining the chord tones and extensions. Use these 1-3-5-7 patterns to get started and then move on to the exercise to get familiar with the extensions.

Am7 with extensions

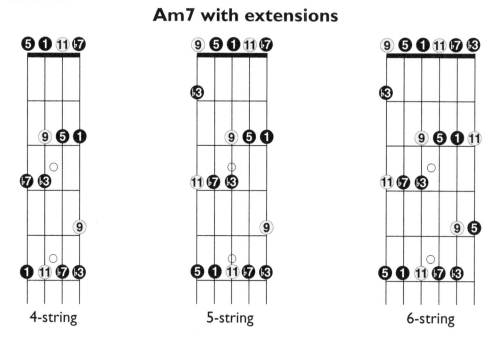

D7 with extensions

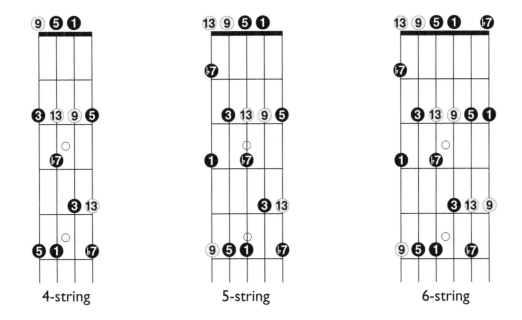

4-string   5-string   6-string

Gmaj7 with extensions

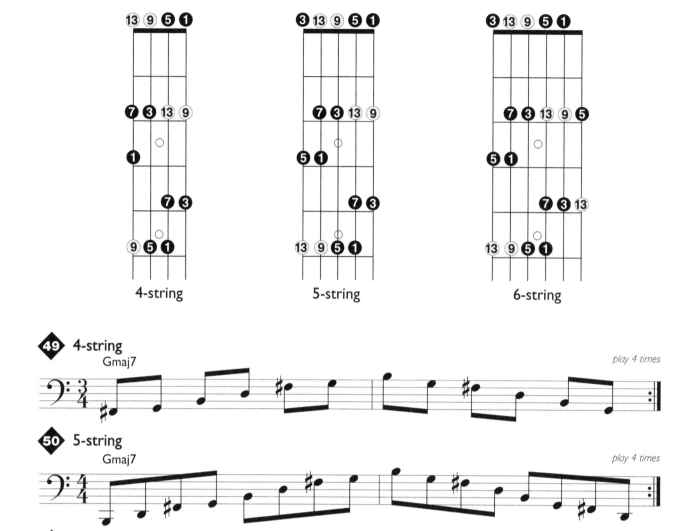

Am7, D7, and Gmaj7 are in the key of G major. For the next example, use a correct extension for every chord. Only one extension is necessary for the two measures of Gmaj7.

...continue

While extensions do a nice job of adding color to an otherwise basic line, they can't be relied upon to reinforce the fundamental sound of the chords. Certain playing situations require a more inventive harmonic approach where a command of extensions are necessary. Other situations might require a more basic approach. Exercise good judgement and consider your role each playing situation.

Review

To make sure you're ready to move on, apply all the exercises we've used to each set of chord changes so far. Here are the ones we've used:

Cm7–F7

Em7–A7

Dm7–G7

Am7–D7–Gmaj7

Here's what we've done with them:

- *Arpeggio lines with direction:* Play four notes of a chord in one direction. As soon as the chord changes, play the nearest chord tone of the next chord in the direction you're going. Keep your line moving in the same direction until you run out of room (within the first five frets).

- *Passing note on beat 4:* Play three consecutive chord tones—then use a passing tone on beat 4. Keep your line in the same direction until you run out of room (within the first five frets).

- *Passing notes on beats 2 and 4:* Any direction within the first five frets.

- *No Roots:* Avoid playing a root on beat 1 of any measure. (any directions).

- *Eighth notes:* Alternate chord tones and passing tones with the eighth note pulse. Fewer roots make it sound "above" the harmony.

- *Direction only:* Play from the lowest note to the highest for each chord. Don't change direction until the highest and lowest available chord tones are reached.

- *Extensions:* Use a correct extension for each chord change. The diagrams on the following pages include chord tones and extensions (in gray) for the first three sets of chord changes.

Cm7 with extensions

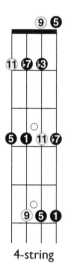
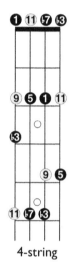
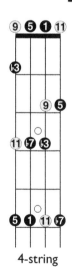

4-string 5-string 6-string

F7 with extensions

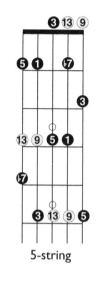
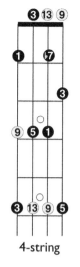
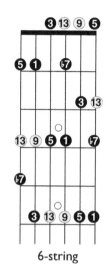

4-string 5-string 6-string

Em7 with extensions

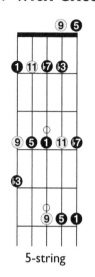
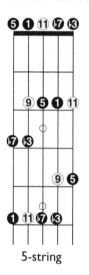
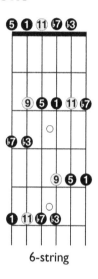

4-string 5-string 6-string

A7 with extensions

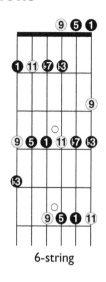
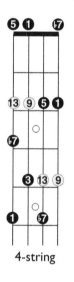
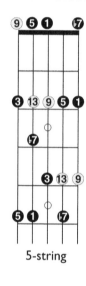
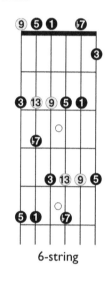

4-string 5-string 6-string

Dm7 with extensions

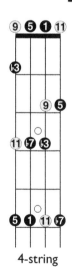
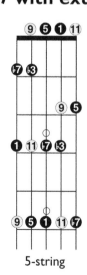
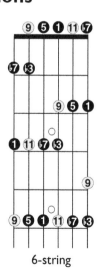

4-string 5-string 6-string

G7 with extensions

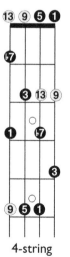
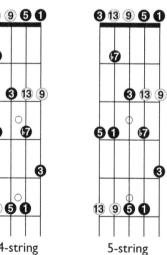
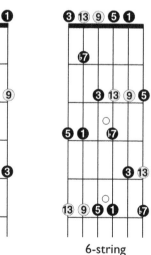

4-string 5-string 6-string

Hand Positions

Key-Finger-String

So far we've spent a lot of time working on harmony within the first five frets. Now we're going to concentrate on a process that will allow you complete control of the entire neck while confining your study to only selected areas of the neck. The reason you decide to locate your hand at any particular location on the neck when you're playing over chord changes should be a result of the harmony. Almost all chord changes imply a key center. Once you decide on a key center, you choose a hand position on the neck where you want to play. The traditional hand position labeling system that uses the fret number where the first finger is located doesn't tell you anything about the key you're in. In order to associate key centers with hand position, since they're related, we're going to use some new terminology. From now on, we'll call the area underneath your fingers in a hand position the "4+2" area. It is defined by assigning each finger to a fret and allowing a stretch to either of the two frets on each side of the established four fret area.

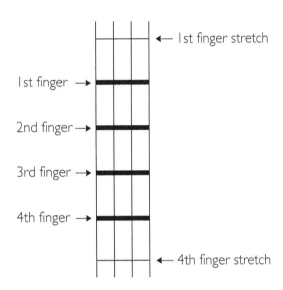

Where do you put your hand when someone asks you to play a G major scale? Most of you will locate your second finger on the third fret (G), E string to play a G major scale. The labeling system that we're going to use takes into account the three decisions that you made for that scale: *"Key – Finger – String."* The label for that position is *"G2E."*

27

Second Finger Position

The most common way of looking at major keys is with the second finger. It usually allows you to play all the notes in a major scale without shifting, which also means you don't have to shift to reach any of the notes of chords within that key. Here's what *G2E* and *C2A* look like:

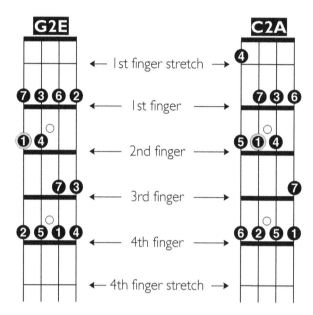

In the rest of the fingerboard diagrams we'll be using, the note on the neck that is used to indicate the hand position will be outlined in gray. If that note happens to be a chord tone it will be filled in with black, otherwise it will be empty.

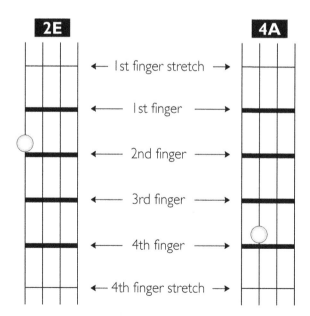

Bm7 and Amaj7

The next exercise uses the key of A major. Here, the location of your hand is A2E (key of A, second finger on the E string). This establishes your 4+2 hand position. We'll use the chord changes Bm7 and Amaj7. Here's what they look like on the neck. The chord tones are black and the extensions are gray.

A2E Bm7 with extensions

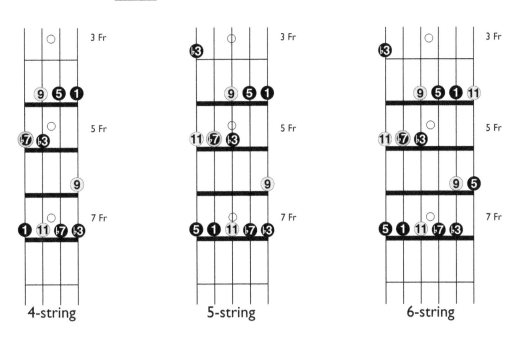

4-string   5-string   6-string

A2E Amaj7 with extensions

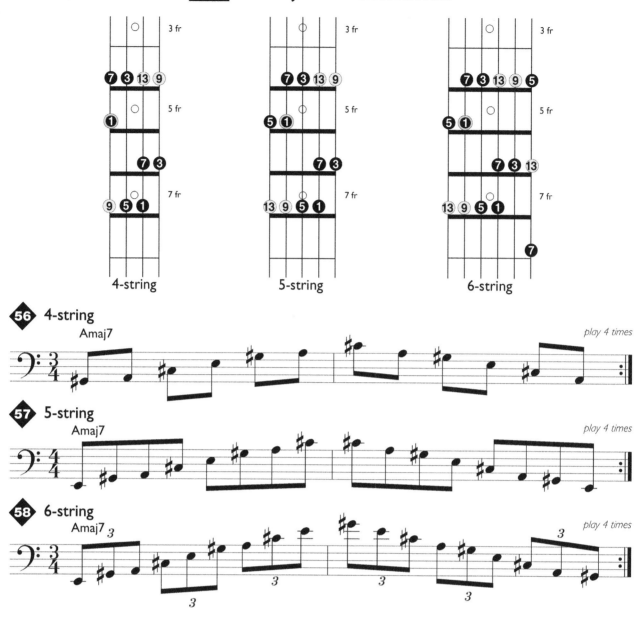

Although the extensions are indicated, just use chord tones 1, 3, 5, and 7 at first. Add the extensions when you're ready. For the next example, use passing tones on beats 2 and 4 and remember to get your passing notes from the key of A when you have a choice.

The fingerings given are for each note within the 4+2 area established by *A2E*. Each note within the main four fret area is played by its corresponding finger. The notes that are one fret on either side of the four fret area (+2) are played by fingers 1 or 4 and are indicated by the "+" after the number. This temporary "stretch" is always immediately followed by a note within the four fret area. For instance, on beat 2 is a B♭ outside the four fret area. By "stretching" with the fourth finger to play that B♭ and then using the fourth finger to play the following A. You immediately return to the finger per fret consistency that allows your hand to "view" the neck. If you play the B♭ with the fourth finger and then play the A with your third finger your hand immediately loses "sight" of the key center. The fingerings that are presented here are very important. If you use them correctly, you'll be able to see the sounds on the neck as consistent shapes anywhere you choose to play on the bass.

Here's a four measure sample line using extensions.

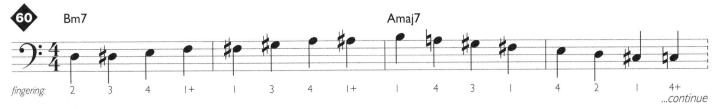

As either of the last two examples ascend or descend you'll notice the notes outside the four fret area ("stretch notes") are played accordingly. Ascending "stretch notes" are played by the first finger and descending "stretch notes" are played by the fourth finger. This allows a smoother return to the four fret area.

Amaj7 – F#m7 – Bm7 – E7

This exercise adds two more chords to the previous one. Since E7 and F#m7 are from the key of A major, we'll use *A2E*. Here's what they look like on the neck. The chord tones are black and the extensions are gray.

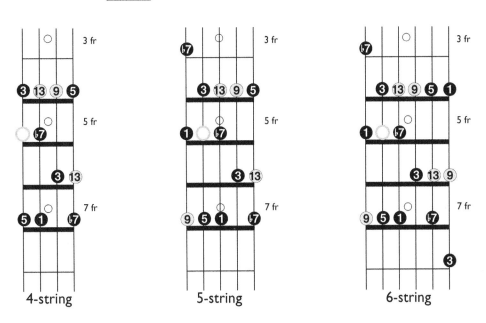

A2E F#m7 with extensions

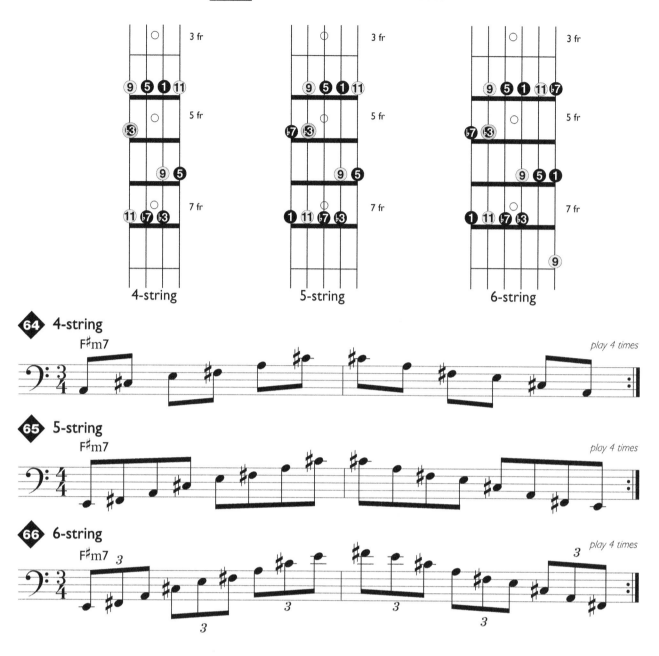

In the next exercise Amaj7, F#m7, Bm7, and E7 last for one measure each. Begin by using just chord tones and passing notes and then move on to extensions when you're ready. This eight measure example uses just chord tones in the first four bars, and extensions in the sec-ond four bars.

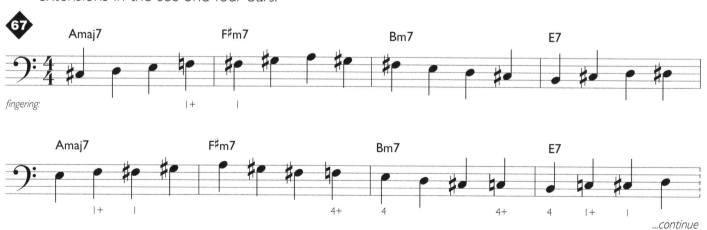

The fingerings provided indicate how to execute the "stretch" notes. The other notes fall within the main four fret area.

Fourth Finger Position

The second most common hand position is the fourth-finger position. It usually requires one stretch outside of the four fret area (to the seventh) to play a major scale. Any chord that includes that seventh scale degree will also involve that stretch.

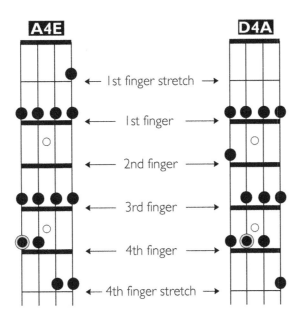

The Connection

Before we get to the A4E exercises, we need to look at how these hand positions connect across the fingerboard. 5- and 6-string basses make it a little easier to see the connection but the following diagrams should make it clear for everyone.

Two to Four

You can connect second finger position to the fourth finger position without shifting. On the left is a second finger position. Next to it is a fourth. In second finger position the octave is played by the 4th finger on the D string. From there you can use a fourth finger hand position. The extra strings that result from a combination of these two positions are provided.

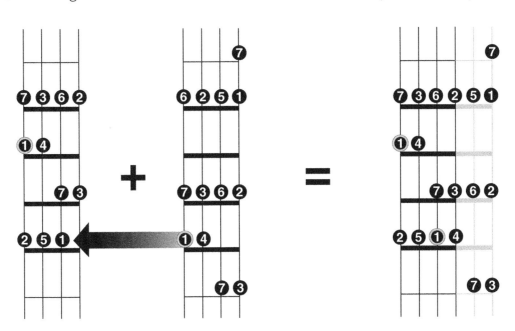

Four to Two

A shift is involved to connect fourth finger to second finger. If you treat fourth finger hand position as a scale then the correct fingering requires that you play the sixth scale degree with the fourth finger which sets up landing on the octave with the second finger. This is the shift that is involved in connecting fourth finger to second finger. The extra strings again are supplied in gray.

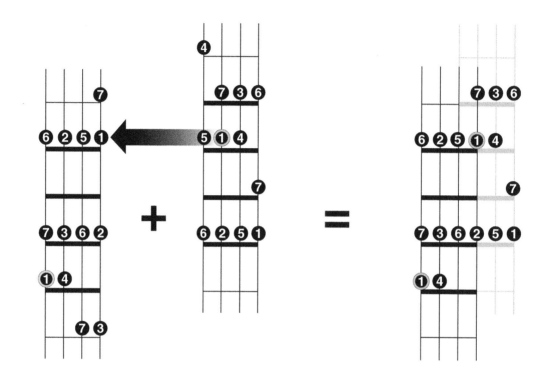

The way these hand positions connect (two to four, four to two) means that no matter where you are on the neck, a combination of two and four will allow you to "see" the key center under your hands. By studying these two hand positions, we're studying information that can be used anywhere on the neck.

Bm7-Amaj7

Although the fourth finger position is less familiar, it is 50% of what you need to know in order to "see" harmony on the neck. The following exercises will use the same key and chord changes as the ones for second finger. The location of your hand is *A4E* (key of A, fourth finger on the E string).

A4E   Bm7 with extensions

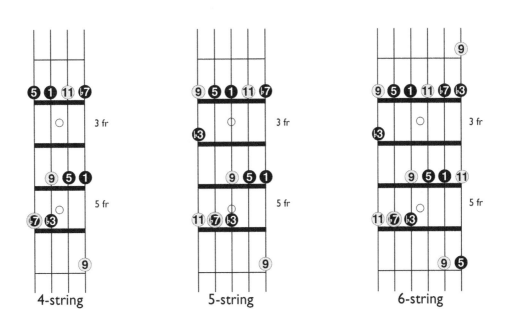

4-string   5-string   6-string

*High F♯ is added so the pattern will loop.

A4E Amaj7 with extensions

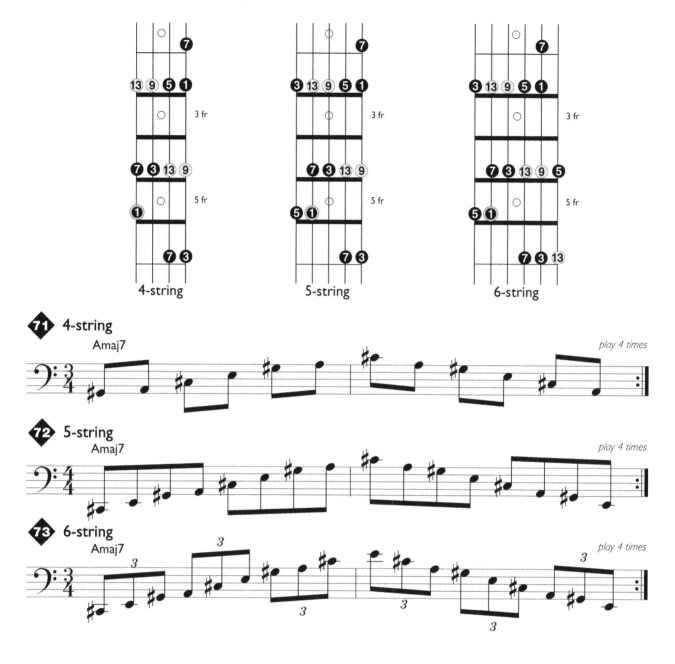

The next exercise uses the connection between fourth finger and second finger.

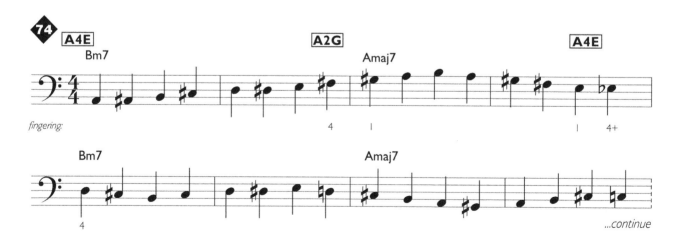

The lower notes of *A4E* are played in that position. Groups of notes on the D string and above should be played in the *A2G* position. The fingerings provided enable you to make the shifts necessary to use the best position.

Amaj7-F#m7-Bm7-E7

Now let's add E7 and F#m7.

A4E **E7 with extensions**

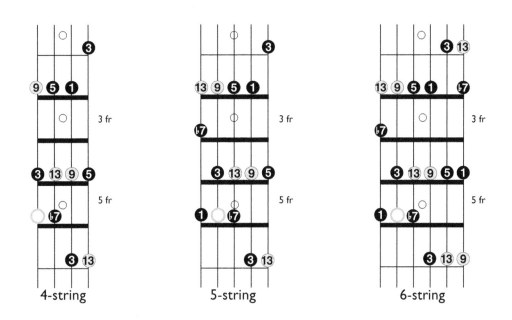

4-string   5-string   6-string

75 **4-string**
E7
play 4 times

76 **5-string**
E7
play 4 times

77 ***6-string**
E7
play 4 times

fingering: 2   1   4   2   4   1   2   4

*Since A4E connects to A2G, fingerings are provided to execute that shift.

A4E F#m7 with extensions

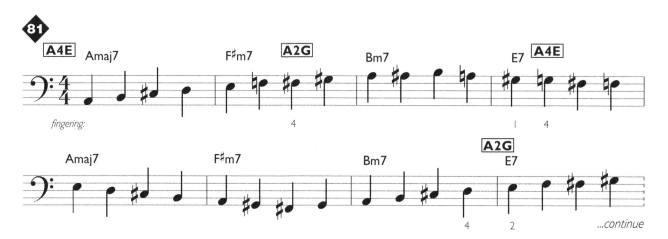

78 4-string

79 5-string

80 *6-string

fingering: | 4 3 | 4 | 3 |

*Fingerings are provided to execute the shift from A4E to A2G.

For the exercise below, use the connection between fourth finger and second finger.

81

A4E Amaj7   F#m7 **A2G** Bm7   E7 **A4E**

fingering: 4 | 4

Amaj7   F#m7   Bm7   **A2G** E7

4 2   ...continue

Your decision to use *A4E* or *A2G* should be based on where you expect your line to go. For instance, in the second measure, if the G# on beat 4 was followed by a F# and continued back down, you'd play the G# with a "stretched" fourth finger and remain in *A4E*. Since it continues higher, it's more comfortable to use the F# to shift into *A2G*.

38

Choosing a Key Center

If a chord progression is put together from chords in the same key, there are consistent relationships between them that give you clues about the key center. As mentioned before, you usually won't see a m7♭5 chord in a major key so you don't have to worry about that one right now. Usually all you need are two chords from the same key and you can figure out the key center from their relationship.

Here are the most important relationships in diatonic harmony:

- The five chord is the only dominant seventh chord. Knowing the location of the fifth will give you the root of the key.

- A major seventh chord only happens on one and four. Two major seventh chords a fourth apart will tell you the lower major seventh chord is the "one" chord.

- A major seventh chord with a minor seventh chord a whole step higher can only happen with the "one" and the "two" chords.

- A major seventh chord and a minor seventh chord a half step lower can only happen with the "four" and "three" chords (keep counting down and you land on the one chord).

- A minor seventh chord with a minor seventh chord a whole step higher can only happen with the "two" and "three" chords.

- The minor seventh chords happen at "two," "three," or "six." If a minor seventh chord is a fourth or a fifth from another minor seventh chord, you have either "three" and "six" or "six" and "two." One more chord is necessary to decide the key.

Here are the chord types in order of their occurrence:

dom7: only happens on the fifth

maj7: happens at "one" and "four"

m7: happens at "two," "three," and "six"

When choosing a key center, first look for a dominant seventh chord. Next look for major seventh chords. A minor seventh chord will tell you the least about a key (since it can be a "two," "three," or "six") but its relationship with other chords helps complete the picture. As soon as you've established a key center you can decide which 4+2 hand position to use to play over those changes.

Choose a key center for the following progressions:

1.	B♭m7	E♭7	A♭maj7	
2.	Am7	Em7	Bm7	
3.	Fmaj7	Am7	B♭maj7	
4.	Fmaj7	Em7	Dm7	
5.	Dmaj7	F♯m7	Bm7	Gmaj7

Answers:

1. B♭m7   E♭7   A♭maj7 = *Key of A♭*
    ii (2)   V (5)   I (1)
    The dominant seventh (E♭) is always a dead giveaway.

2. Am7   Em7   Bm7 = *Key of G*
    ii (2)   vi (6)   iii (3)
    Two minor sevenths a whole step apart (Am7 and Bm7) are "two" and "three."

3. Fmaj7   Am7   B♭maj7 = *Key of F*
    I (1)   iii (3)   IV (4)
    Two major sevenths a fourth apart (Fmaj7 and B♭maj7) are "one" and "four," also a major seventh chord with a minor seventh a half step below (B♭maj7 and Am7) are "four" and "three."

4. Fmaj7   Em7   Dm7 = *Key of C*
    IV (4)   iii (3)   ii (2)
    Two minor sevenths a whole step apart (Em7 and Dm7) are "two" and "three," also a major seventh chord with a m7 a half step below (Fmaj7 and Em7) are "four" and "three."

5. Dmaj7   F♯m7   Bm7   Gmaj7 = *Key of D*
    I (1)   iii (3)   vi (6)   IV (4)
    Two major sevenths a fourth apart (Gmaj7 and Dmaj7) are "one" and "four."

Finding More Than One Key

When a progression contains more that one key center, the correct hand position can make playing the progression easier. For example, the following progression can be played in one 4+2 location on the neck even though it involves more than one key center.

Ebm7   Ab7   Dbmaj7   Cm7   F7   Bbmaj7

The first three chords are in the key of Db major. (2, 5, and 1). The last three chords are in the key of Bb major (2, 5, and 1). *Db2A* (key of Db, 2nd finger on the A string) works for the first three chords and *Bb4E* (key of Bb, fourth finger on the E string) works for the last three chords. The whole progression can be played in one place on the neck without shifting.

The following chord progressions involve more than one key center. Choose a 4+2 hand position for each key center. The hand positions should share the same location on the neck.

1.	Em7	A7	Dmaj7	Dm7	G7	Cmaj7
2.	Abmaj7	Dbmaj7	Cm7	F7	Bbmaj7	
3.	Dmaj7	C#m7	Cmaj7	Bm7		

Answers:

1.	**D4A** Em7 ii (2)	A7 V (5)	Dmaj7 I (1)	**C2A** Dm7 ii (2)	G7 V (5)	Cmaj7 I (1)
2.	**Ab2E** Abmaj7 I (1)	Dbmaj7 IV (4)	**Bb4E** Cm7 iii/ii (3/2)	F7 V (5)	Bbmaj7 I (1)	
3.	**A4E** Dmaj7 IV (4)	C#m7 iii (3)	**G2E** Cmaj7 IV (4)	Bm7 iii (3)		

The next two exercises involve different key centers but can be played in one location on the neck. Remember, the first thing to do when faced with a new set of chord changes is analyze them for key center and hand position. Here's the first progression:

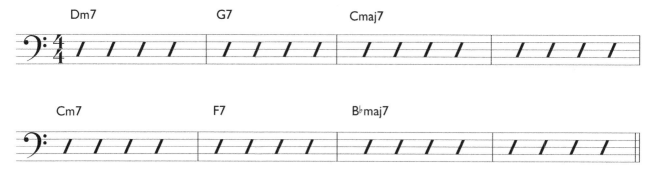

Since hand position is part of your analysis, you don't have to label individual chords that are in the same key. Just use the 4+2 label to indicate your decision.

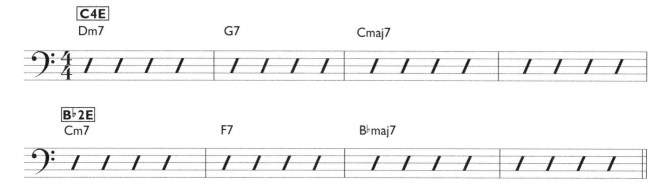

C4E   indicates that you've decided that *Dm7, G7, and Cmaj7* is a 2-5-1 in *C*.

B♭2E   indicates that you've decided that *Cm7, F7, and B♭maj7* is a 2-5-1 in *B♭*.

Dm7–G7–Cmaj7–Cm7–F7–B♭maj7

For this exercise refer to pages 45 and 46 for the fingerboard diagrams to these chords. Use chord tones and extensions on beats 1 and 3, passing notes on 2 and 4. Remember to play passing tones from the key if you have a choice, and use your first finger for ascending "stretch" notes and fourth finger for descending "stretch" notes. Fingerings are given to help you maintain hand position.

...continue

The empty bars are provided in case you need to write out a line to get started. Just make sure you do most of your work while looking at the neck. Since the bass fingerboard is symmetric, the visual reinforcement you get from working with the shapes on the fingerboard allow you to move those shapes around and play comfortably anywhere on the neck.

Cm7–D♭maj7–Cm7–F7–B♭maj7

This progression introduces two chords we haven't worked with so far—the "three"-chord and "four"-chord:

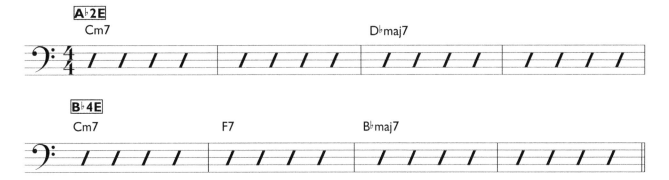

The "Three"-Chord

A♭2E and *B♭4E* allow you to stay in one location to play the whole progression. The Cm7 in measure 1 is a the "three"-chord of A♭ major. If you look ahead to the chord diagrams on pages 45 and 46 you'll notice the "three"-chords only include the eleventh as an extension. Normally, the 9th works on minor seventh chords but the ninth that comes from the key is a ♭9. In this case it would be a D♭ against a Cm7—not a pretty sound. When you use the natural ninth over a "three"-chord it gives you a note that is not in the key. In this case it would be a D natural. Using it on a strong beat would definitely imply another key center, which is not a bad idea when you're working on improvisation. For now, avoid the ninth of a "three"-chord.

The "four"-chord

Dbmaj7 is the "four"-chord of Ab. What's different about the "four"-chord is that all three extensions (the ninth, eleventh, and thirteenth) can be effectively used on strong beats. Normally the natural eleventh of a major seventh chord sounds awful. The eleventh of a "four"-chord is a sharp eleventh which doesn't conflict with the chord the way the natural eleventh does. As with all extensions, the sharp eleventh doesn't reinforce the basics of the chord, but it does add color to the sound of a line. You might have been taught that sharp elevenths will work over any major seventh chord. When you use a sharp eleventh over a "one"-chord, you're implying the sound of a different key. Again, this is a good improvisation choice, but keep your focus on the current key center until you're ready to move on.

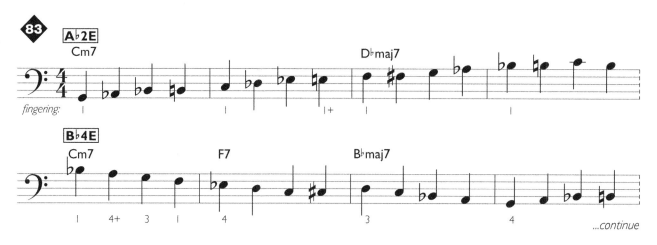

In this example the sharp eleventh of the "four"-chord is used in measure 3. In measure 5 the line stays in Bb4E position by stretching to the A with the fourth finger. You could also play the four notes of measure 5 in Bb2G position (fingering 2-1-4-2). While either fingering works, you should consider Bb2G as the upper part of Bb4E and always use the lowest label for analyzing. Remember to shift while on the upper strings if necessary.

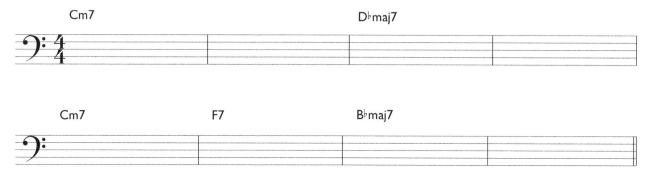

The following pages provide all the diagrams you'll need for chords in second and fourth finger positions. The diagrams are based on the E string but are moveable to any string. All you have to remember is how second finger position and fourth finger position connect to each other. For instance, if you're in a C4E position, the notes on upper strings require a shift to C2G. You don't have to write the C2G label, just remember that it's part of C4E. If you have a 5- or 6-string bass, an F4A position should be labeled F2B since they connect without shifting. It's best to use the label from the lower strings and visualize the connection to upper positions. Refer to these pages to get a "look" at what any particular chord looks like for the rest of the exercises in this book.

2E "one"-chord (maj7) with extensions

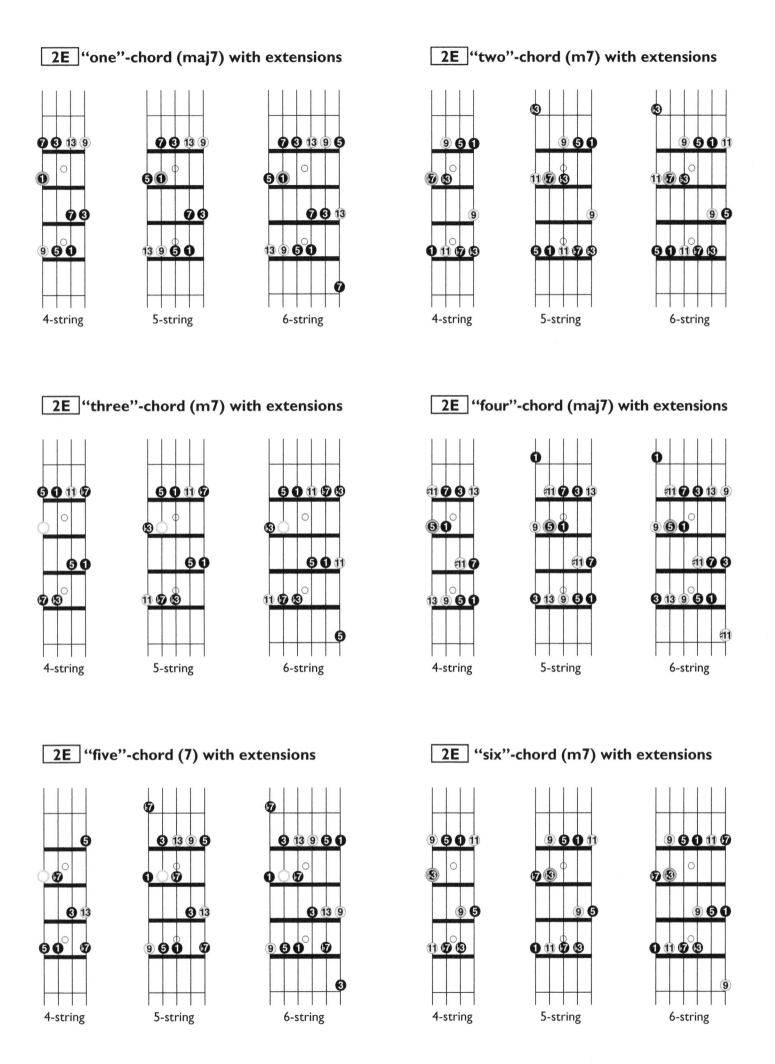

2E "two"-chord (m7) with extensions

2E "three"-chord (m7) with extensions

2E "four"-chord (maj7) with extensions

2E "five"-chord (7) with extensions

2E "six"-chord (m7) with extensions

4-string 5-string 6-string

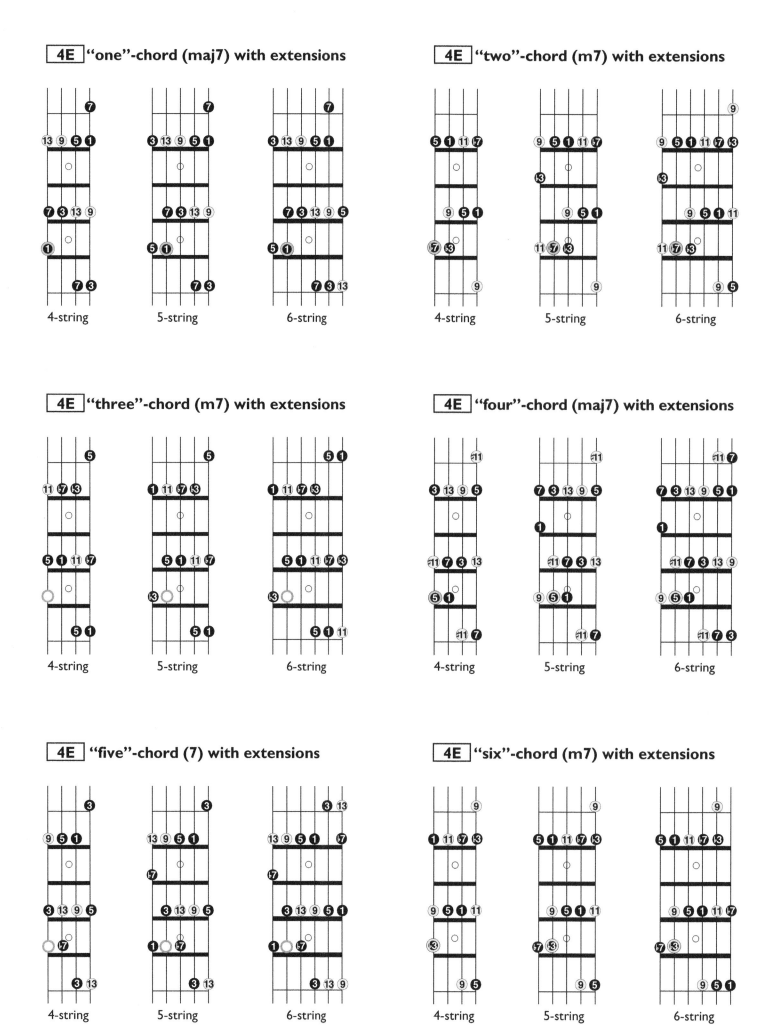

46

Minor

So far we've confined our study of the neck to major key centers. Even though we've had some key changes and secondary dominant chords, it's all been major diatonic harmony. The next step is minor key centers.

Just like major, there are two hand positions for minor keys. You probably know the keys of C major and A minor are related. Major and minor hand positions are related the same way. For instance, the same notes from *C2A* and *C4E* will give you *Am4E* and *Am1E* :

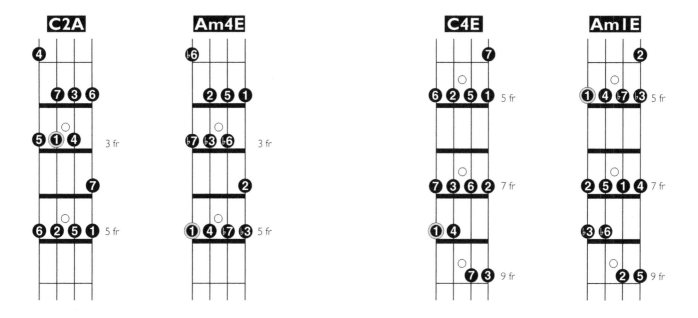

The connections between the two minor hand positions are similar to the major positions. The fourth finger position connects to the first without a shift:

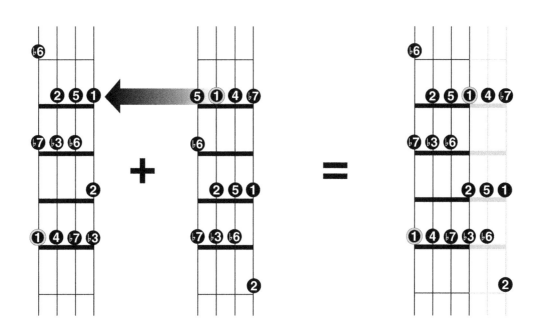

The first finger position connects to the fourth with a half-step shift:

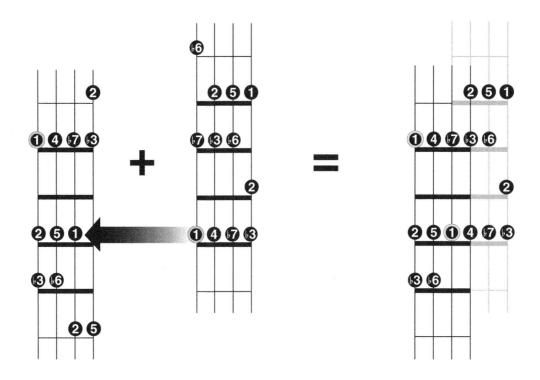

Here are the kinds of chords and their chord tones/extensions that occur in a minor key:

"one"-chord	m7	1, ♭3, 5, ♭7, 9, 11
"two"-chord	m7♭5	1, ♭3, ♭5, ♭7, 9, ♭13
"three"-chord	maj7	1, 3, 5, 7, 9, 13
"four"-chord	m7	1, ♭3, 5, ♭7, 9, 11
"five"-chord	dom7(♭9)	1, 3, 5, ♭7, ♭9, ♭13
"six"-chord	maj7	1, 3, 5, 7, 9, ♯11, 13
"seven"-chord	dom7	1, 3, 5, ♭7, ♭9, ♭13

The "two"-chord: m7♭5

The minor seven flat five is different than the chords we've studied so far. The chord tones 1, ♭3, ♭5, and ♭7 of the minor seven flat five are self explanatory, what's different are the extensions. On a regular minor seven chord the correct extensions to use are nine and eleven. For the minor seven flat five, the eleventh and flat thirteenth sound best.

The reason the ninth doesn't work over a minor seven flat five is because the ninth that comes from the key is a flat ninth. While the flat ninth sounds good over the "five"-chord, it doesn't work nearly as well as the eleven and flat thirteenth. The natural nine is often recommended over a minor seven flat five. It doesn't reinforce the sound of the key but it's a good improvising choice because of the tension it creates by implying another key. The reason the flat thirteenth works is because it doesn't conflict with the seventh or the flat fifth. Put it down an octave and you can see it's a whole step from either one.

The "five"-chord: 7♭9

The other chord you need to pay attention to in a minor key is the "five"-chord. It uses a chord tone that is not from the key signature. For instance, since the key of A minor has no sharps or flats, the "five"- chord should be minor seventh (E, G, B, D). Instead it is E7 (E, G♯, B, D). Almost all minor progressions use a dominant seventh chord for the "five"-chord. The "five"-chord in A minor is E7 and has a G♯ that's not from the key.

The "five"-chord in minor is also different because it uses a flat ninth, and flat thirteenth for the correct extensions. When you play over the "five"-chord in minor, you need to slightly alter the half step/whole step process we've been using. The flat nine causes the problem. The distance between E and G♯ is a major third. Normally the passing note would be F♯, but that's not in the key. Using the F natural as the passing note helps reinforce the minor key sound. It creates a minor third (G♯ to F) within the half-step/whole-step line, but it sounds much better. The symbol for the "five"-chord in minor is always followed by the flat ninth (E7♭9) which makes minor key centers easier to recognize when you're analyzing chord progressions.

Just like in a major key center, the chords you'll see most often in a minor key center are chords "one" through "six." Of these, the minor seven flat five "two"-chord is the only fingerboard shape we haven't looked at. Here's what it looks like in the *Cm1A* hand position.

Cm1A "two"-chord (Dm7♭5) with extensions

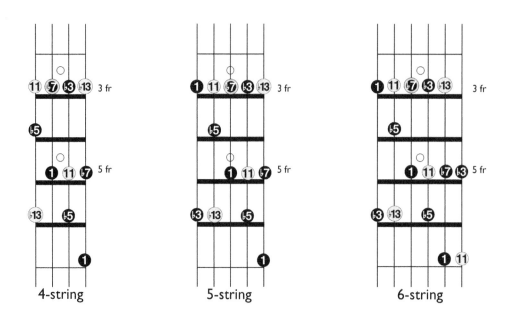

4-string   5-string   6-string

Cm7-Fm7-Dm7♭5-G7♭9

Here's an exercise in the *Cm1A* hand position using the previously mentioned minor seven flat five and seven flat nine, as well as the "one"-chord and "four" chord in minor. These chords are the most common for minor progressions. It is less likely you'll see the "three," "six," or "seven" in a minor progression.

...continue

Notice in measure 6 the eleventh and flat thirteenth are used over the Dm7♭5. Measure 7 is an example of when to break the half-step/whole-step rules over the "five"-chord in minor. The minor third between the B and A♭ create a more "minor" sounding line than using an A natural on beat 2.

The notes in measure 16 bring up an interesting thing about seven flat nine chords. The flat nine on a dominant allows you to treat a dominant seventh chord as "altered." Altered means you can use ♭9, ♯9, ♭5, and ♯5. In measure 16 the sharp nine is played on beats 1 and 3. If you choose to treat flat nine chords as altered, use your ear and carefully choose the notes that resolve the tension these extensions can create. Usually the sharp nine sounds best when it resolves to the 5th of the following "one" chord. The flat thirteen sounds best resolving to the ninth or eleventh of the following "one" chord. In order to develop a sense of where these extensions want to resolve, practice playing each extension as a whole note on the second bar of G7♭9 and listen for which chord tone it wants to resolve to. Then try to get your lines to accomplish the same thing.

The next exercise uses the same progression in the *Cm4E* hand position.

Cm4E "two"-chord (Dm7♭5) with extensions

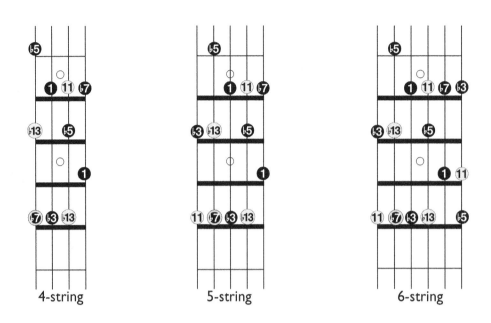

4-string   5-string   6-string

88 **4-string**
Dm7♭5
play 4 times

89 **5-string**
Dm7♭5
play 4 times

90 **6-string**
Dm7♭5
play 4 times

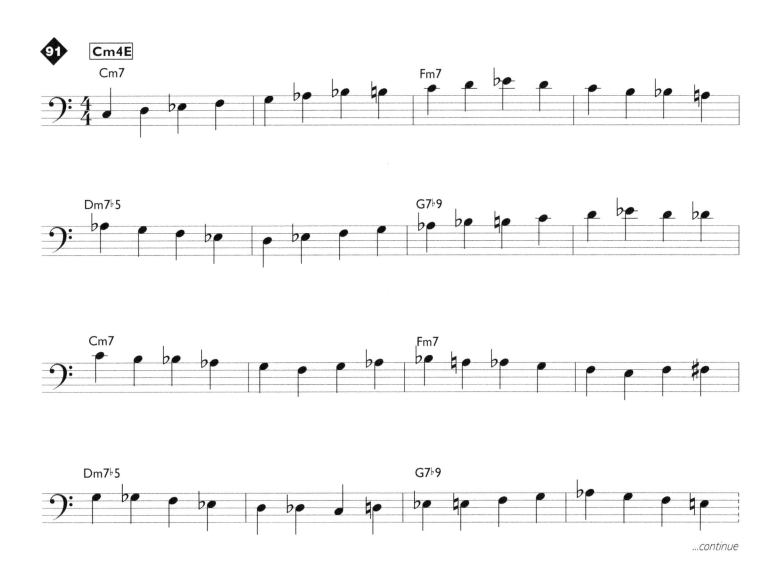

...continue

In measure 7 the flat nine and the major third are used with the sharp nine as a passing tone on beat 2. The eleventh is used over Fm7 in measures 4 and 11 and over Dm7♭5 in measure 13. In measure 15 the flat thirteen and in measure 16 the flat nine are used over the G7♭9 chord.

Bm7♭5–E7♭9–Am7–Dm7–G7–Cmaj7

This next exercise combines the connections across the fingerboard using the major and minor hand positions. The first three chords are in A minor and the last three are in C major. By beginning in *Am1E,* you can use its related major hand position, *C4E.* Both positions require a shift to play the notes on the upper strings. Refer to pages 34 and 48 for the connection diagrams. Remember, the shift to the upper position *(Am4D and C2G)* is dictated by how many notes you plan to play in the upper position. You may not be able to decide right away, but eventually you'll learn to anticipate how long your line will stay in either position.

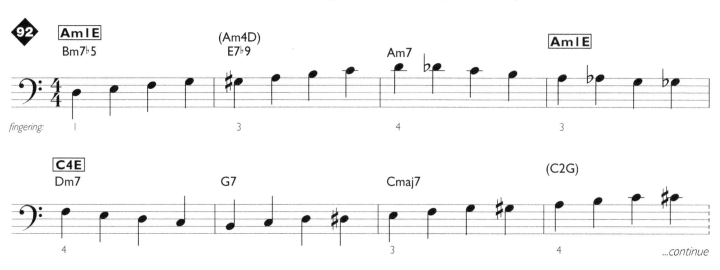

The upper hand position is shown in parentheses. For *Am1E* the shift occurs so measures 2 and 3 can be comfortably played in *Am4D,* then returns to *Am1E* for the fourth measure. For *C4E* the shift only occurs on the last measure. If you continue playing from measure 8 to the next Bm7♭5 chord, you will be in *Am4D* until the notes descend into the lower position. Remember, since the main label comes from the lower position, the upper position is shown in parentheses.

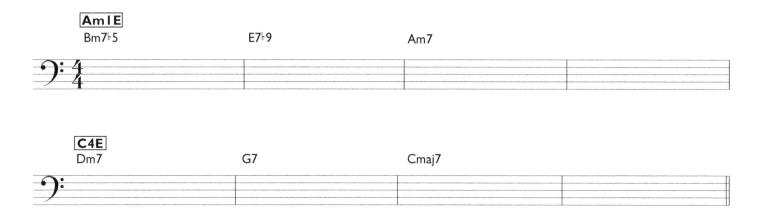

Shifting

The first thing to do when choosing a hand position for any progression is analyze the progression for key centers. Once you've found the basic key center (or key centers), you can easily locate a position that makes the harmony easy to see and keeps your hand from aimlessly following the roots around. The goal is to eliminate as much shifting as possible. This enables you to learn more about information that can be transferred and used for other progressions.

Occasionally some shifting is inevitable, since one position doesn't always work for an entire progression. Fortunately, these hand positions allow you to change key centers without ever shifting more that a half step. For instance, here's how you can get from the key of C (C2E) to every other key center.

KEY OF C	NEW KEY	NEW POSITION	SHIFT
C2E	D♭	D♭2E	1/2 up
C2E	D	D4E	None
C2E	E♭	E♭4E	1/2 up
C2E	E	E2A	1/2 down
C2E	F	F2A	None
C2E	G♭	G♭2A	1/2 up
C2E	G	G4A	None
C2E	A♭	A♭4A	1/2 up
C2E	A	A2D	1/2 down
C2E	B♭	B♭2D	None
C2E	B	B2E	1/2 down

For shifting practice, supply the answers to the following chart. The left column is the key center/hand position. Write the corresponding hand position label for the key in the right column that is a half-step shift away. Indicate whether the shift is up or down in the middle column. The first answer is given.

FROM	HALF STEP SHIFT	TO
G major G2E	Down	B major B2A
C minor C1A		A major
A major A2E		F minor
D major D4E		E major
G major G4A		B♭ minor

Answers:

FROM	HALF STEP SHIFT	TO
G major **G2E**	Down	B major **B2A**
C minor **C1A**	Up	A major **A2E**
A major **A2E**	Up or Down	F minor **Fm4A (up)** or **Fm1D**
D major **D4E**	Down	E major **E2A**
G major **G4A**	Down	B♭ minor **B♭m1E**

Am7-Bm7-Cm7-Dm7-E♭m7-F7♭9-Fm7-B♭7

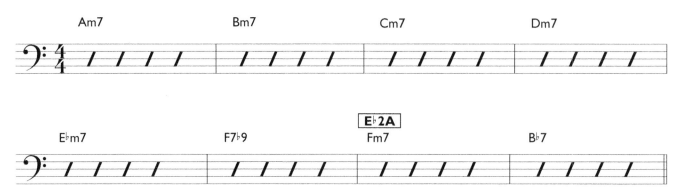

This exercise involves using half-step shifts to get to four different key centers.

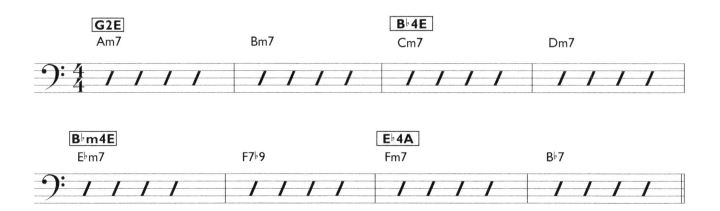

From *G2E* to *B♭4E* shift is a half step up.

From *B♭4E* to *B♭m4E* requires no shift.

From *B♭m4E* to *E♭4A* requires no shift.

From *E♭4A* to *G2E* shift is a half step down.

Remember, if you have a 5- or 6-string bass, *E♭4A* should be *E♭2B*

The next progression is higher on the difficulty level than we've been doing so far, so the track's tempo is a little slower. Remember to avoid the ninth of the "three"-chord and get passing notes from the key center when you can.

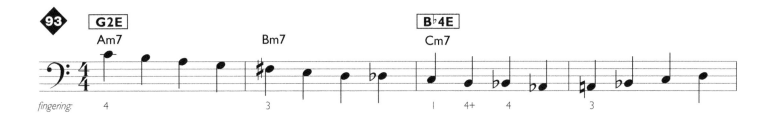

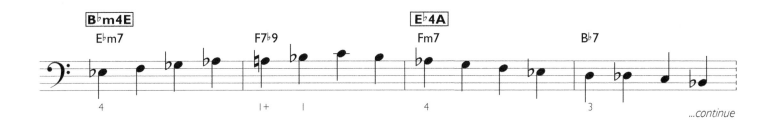

...continue

Memorizing

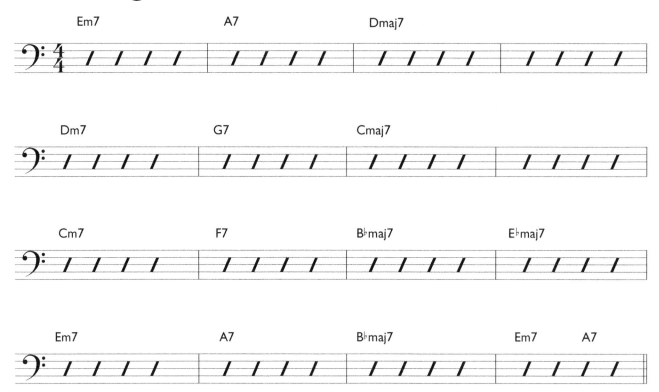

Knowing the neck well means being able to "see" different key centers under your hand. In order to teach your hand to "see" the fingerboard, you should be looking at the neck and not the paper. Your ability to memorize chord changes instead of reading them becomes a valuable asset during this process.

The following progression has fifteen chord changes. Memorizing this progression as a series of chord changes is like memorizing a thirty-seven digit phone number:

Em7–A7–Dmaj7–Dm7–G7–Cmaj7–Cm7–F7–B♭maj7–
E♭maj7–Em7–A7–B♭maj7–Em7–A7

An easier way to memorize chord changes is by function. For instance, this progression has three key centers: D, C, and B♭. In each key there is a 2-5-1. The 2-5-1s take up seventy-five percent of the progression. By connecting what happens in each key you can reduce what you have to memorize by fifty percent and have information that can transfer to any key and to other tunes. Here's how it works.

First, write what happens in the first key:

2 5 1

Now you need a way to connect it to the next key which is a whole step down. Instead of writing instructions to the next key center and then to the new chord (two steps), just give yourself the interval to get from the last chord in one key to the first chord in the next key (only one step). In this case the root doesn't move so use the word "becomes."

2 5 1 becomes

The same thing happens in the next line. Instead of writing it again, add 2x's (2 times).

2 5 I becomes 2x's

The same thing happens in the next line with the addition of a "four"-chord. The interval to the next root is a half step up.

2 5 I becomes 2x's

2 5 I 4 $\frac{1}{2}$↑

In the next key is a 2-5. Then up a half step to a "one"-chord, a tri-tone to a short 2-5 and you're back where you started.

2 5 I becomes 2x's

2 5 I 4 $\frac{1}{2}$↑

2 5 $\frac{1}{2}$↑ I TT 2 5

Using this method to store the information on your brain's hard drive takes up less room and allows you to play it in any key. Also, it closely relates to hand position information so what you learn about this tune will apply to other similar progressions. Here are the hand positions for this exercise:

| D2A |
2 5 I becomes

| C4E |
2 5 I becomes

| B♭2E |
2 5 I 4 $\frac{1}{2}$↑

| D2A | | B♭2E | | D2A |
2 5 $\frac{1}{2}$↑ I TT 2 5

In order to memorize this progression, play along with the track just using roots from the three hand positions. Then play through it using just half notes (root-fifth, root-third, etc.) In order to see if you have it memorized, try starting in another key (like A♭) and play through it with just roots (don't worry about position). If you end up where you started you probably realize how valuable this memory process is—you can use it in any key!

Once you have it memorized, practice a conventional bass line and work your way up to the whole-step/half-step process that we've been doing. *Do not* write down a line and *do not* read the written progression on page 58. You can hear an example of a line that uses these three hand positions at the beginning of track 94, but in keeping with the spirit if the exercise, it's not written out.

Secondary Dominants

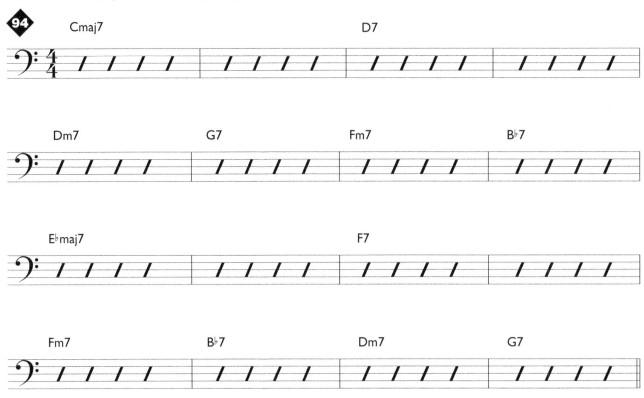

The first thing to look for when analyzing a chord progression is a dominant seventh chord. The first dominant seventh in measure 3 (D7) is not from the key of C. Therefore, we could say the key for those two measures is G major. Since it's an isolated dominant seventh chord (the chords before and after it are not in that key) you can keep it a part of C major by calling it a secondary dominant. A secondary dominant is the five of a chord in a key other than the "one"-chord. In this case it's the five of five, which is the most common secondary dominant. To keep things simple, we'll call it a 2^7. Here's how to memorize the progression.

I			**2⁷**	
2	**5**	2↓	**2**	**5**
I			**2⁷**	
2	**5**	maj3↑	**2**	**5**

Treating the D7 as a secondary dominant makes analyzing and memorizing the progression easier, but playing it requires an extra step. Although D7 indirectly belongs to the key of C, your hand needs to "see" the notes from G major (D7 is the five of G). The basic guideline is that the notes for a secondary dominant come from the key that it implies. For instance, a five of six in the Key of C (E7) would imply notes from the key of A minor. Since D7 is the five of a dominant chord, it's considered part of the key of G major.

Here's the progression analyzed for hand positions.

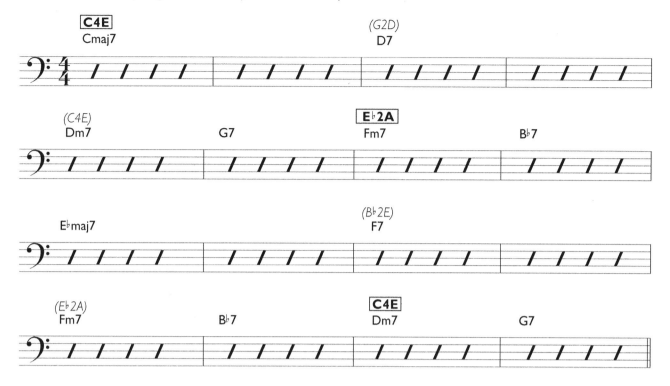

By starting with *C4E* you're able to use *E♭2A* without shifting. The *(G2D)* in measure 3 is a *(G4B)* for 5- and 6-string basses. If you're playing *G2D* on a 4-string bass, it's best to see notes on the E string as part of an imaginary *G4B*. The A-, D-, and G-string notes still come from *G2D*. Here's the first sixteen measures of track 94.

...continue

The next exercise is a good way to see if you're really in command of your hand positions. It starts in *C2A*, goes as high as *E♭2E* and returns to *C2A* in the last two measures. The largest shift allowed is three frets from one position to another. The idea is to start with notes within the first five frets, play notes above the twelfth fret and return to the first five frets by the end of the progression.

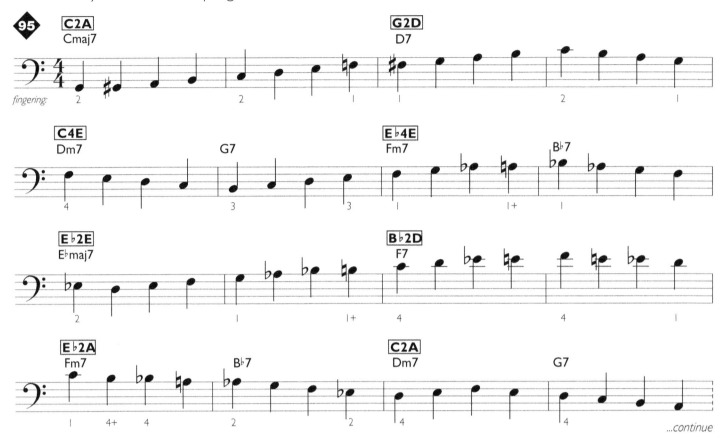

Sometimes the sequence of notes and fingerings will allow you to anticipate the next position by one beat. In measure 2 the F played by the first finger doesn't belong in *C2A* but it is a 1+ of *G2D*. By playing the E, F, and F♯ with the first finger, the transition to *G2D* is made smoother. Similar transitions occur from measure 5-6 and from 12-13. Here are the changes and hand positions.

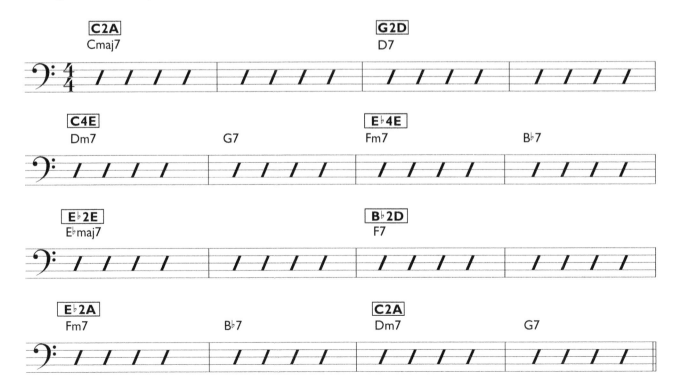

Three/Four

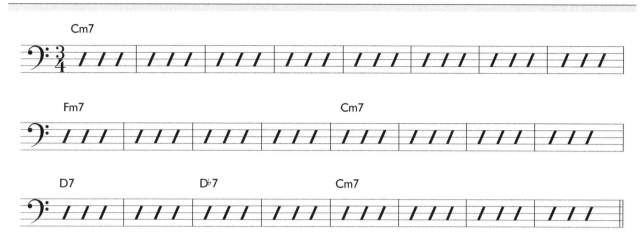

Playing in 3/4 presents a different strong beat/weak beat scheme than we've worked on so far. In a measure of 3/4 the strong beat is still 1. Beat 2 is considered almost as strong as 1, while 3 is the weak beat. The note you choose for beat 2 (the semi-strong beat) is based on the distance to the next chord tone or extension on beat 1 of the next measure and the passing note choices in between. For example, in the first bar on the next page, starting on a C and ascending, the next chord tone is E♭. You don't have a choice here, D♭ and D work for beats 2 and 3. From the E♭ in measure 2 to the G on beat 1 of measure 3, you have a choice of notes to use to get there. Treating beat 2 as a strong beat when you have a choice will put an F on beat 2 and an F♯ on beat 3. You can hear that this is a better choice than an E on 2 and an F on beat 3. Since we already have the "minor thirds rule" for 4/4, this could be called the "major thirds rule" for 3/4. When the chord tones on beat 1 are a major third apart, use a chord tone or correct extension on beat 2 and a passing note on beat 3.

The harmony in this progression is fairly static (chords lasting for more that 2 measures.) This exercise is going to focus on a way to help create more interest over these static sounding changes by using "implied harmony". By implying dominant chords in the right places, you can establish movement and phrasing that makes your lines flow better. In this progression the fourth measure of each four-bar phrase is where the implied dominant chord works.

You choose the "five"-chord of the chord that starts the next four bar phrase. For example, The G7♭9 in measure 4, breaks up the eight consecutive measures of Cm7 into two four-bar phrases. By implying a C7♭9 on measure 8, you create a stronger sense of arriving at Fm7. There is only one note difference between the chord tones and extension of Cm7 and Fm7. The C7♭9 helps separate the sound of Cm7 from Fm7 and makes the beginning of the next four-bar phrase stronger. Here's the progression with the implied chords in parentheses:

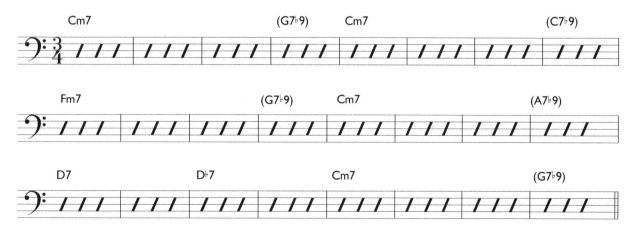

Since the chords last so long, don't worry about labeling the hand positions before you start this exercise. Use half steps and whole steps for your line, but switch to arpeggios for the implied "five"-chords. Also, make sure that your arpeggios include the third of the chord. Here's a sample line for the first twenty-four measures of track 96.

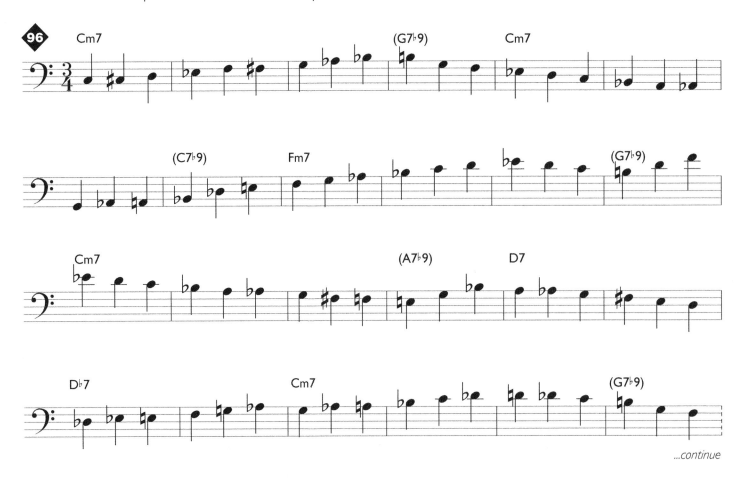

...continue

If you analyze this progression for hand positions, you'll find that the chords (D7 and Db7) are not in the key of C minor. Since we just finished with secondary dominants, the D7 should look familiar. It's the "five" of five. For these two measures, use a G major hand position.

The Db7 is not a secondary dominant because it is not a "five" of any chord from the key of C minor. It's called a "tritone sub" (substitute). A tritone is another name for a diminished fifth. Three (tri) whole steps from G is Db. The Db7 is used as a substitute for G7. Here's how the the tritone sub works: The most important chord tones of any chord, besides the root, are the third and seventh. The third and seventh of G7 are B and F. When G7 resolves to Cm7. The chord tones B and F resolve to C and Eb. The Db7 chord also has B and F as chord tones, as the seventh and third. These same two chord tones resolve the same way to Cm7. The only difference is the root.

The tritone sub creates an interesting hand position situation. Since Db7 is the "five"-chord of Gb, your hand position should be based on Gb major. But, since it's also a tritone sub for G, you should use G natural as a passing tone between F and Ab. You can also use G natural as a sharp eleven extension. You can always recognize tritone subs because they usually resolve down one half step.

This next exercise focuses more on shifting. Remember, the first thing you should do when you see a new progression is analyze it for key center/hand positions. The example below uses minor and major key centers.

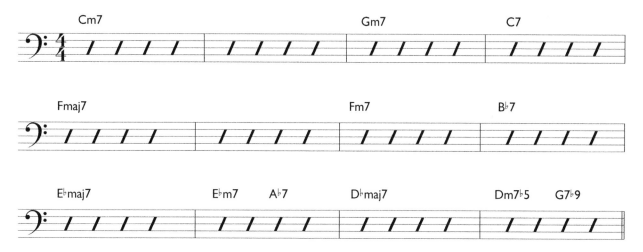

Except for the last few exercises, we've tried to keep most of the shifting to a minimum in order to focus on what's under your hands. In the next exercise, we're going to work on moving around more. By starting in *Cm1A, Cm4E,* and *Cm1E,* you can play through this progression by only moving your hand positions a half step.

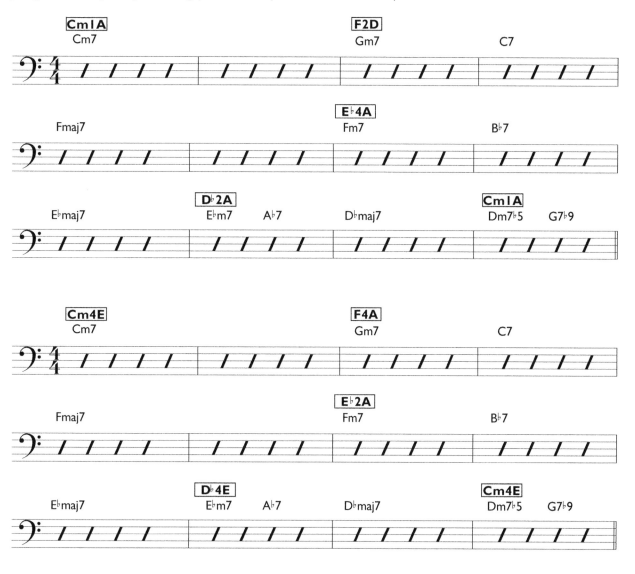

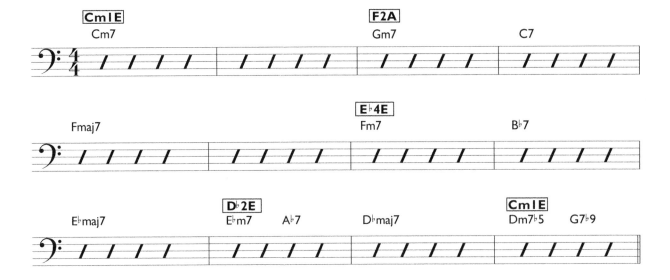

Practice playing through the progression with each of these starting positions *(Cm1A, Cm4E,* and *Cm1E)* This will prepare you for the next exercise: playing smoothly from *Cm1A* to *Cm1E* and back every twenty-four measures. Here are the hand positions to use.

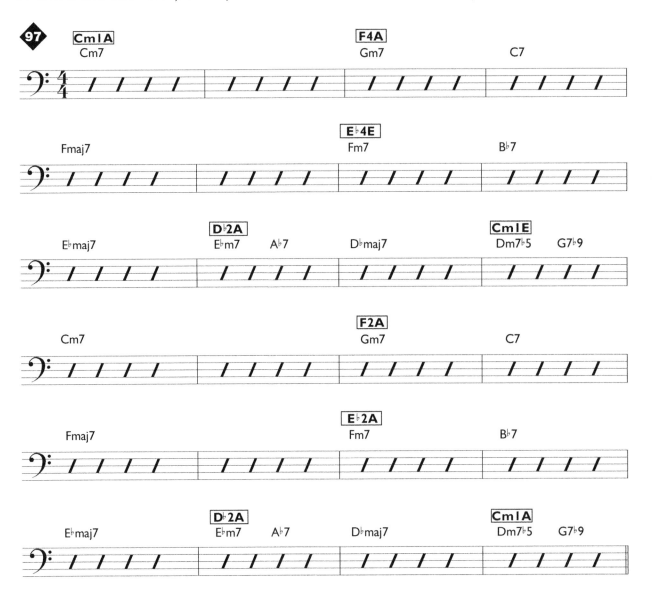

Here's the first 24 measures of track 98.

The fingerings are provided to show the transitions between positions:

- Measure 2, beat 4: third finger anticipates the move to *F4A*
- Measure 6, beat 4: first finger makes the transition to *E♭4E*
- Measure 14, beat 4: first finger anticipates the move to *F2A*
- Measure 18: You could actually play from A♭ on beat 2 to the F in measure 19 all with the fourth finger. It's not politically correct fingering but it gets the job done.
- Measure 21, beat 4: fourth finger makes the transition to *D♭2A*

Other Chords

All the chords we've worked on so far have been part of major or minor key centers. Most of the other types of chord symbols you'll see fall into the familiar major seventh, minor seventh and dominant seventh categories. Here's a list of most of the other kinds of chord symbols you'll see and how to treat them. They're all listed with a G root.

Major

Gmaj9	same as maj7, emphasize ninth
Gmaj13	same as maj7, emphasize thirteenth
Gmaj7($\sharp$11)	treat as a "four" chord in a major key (sharp eleven occurs naturally)
Gmaj7$\sharp$5	same as maj7, emphasize sharp five, use natural five on weak beat
G6/9	same as maj7, emphasize ninth and sixth, use major seven on weak beat
G6	same as maj7, except emphasize 6th and use major seven on weak beat

Minor

Gm9	same as m7, emphasize ninth
Gm11	same as m7, emphasize eleventh
Gm13	same as m7, emphasize thirteenth
Gm6/9	same as m7, emphasize sixth and ninth
Gm7$\sharp$5	same as m7, emphasize sharp five, use natural five on weak beat, also thought of as inversion: E$\flat$maj7/G

Dominant

G+7	treat as "five" of C minor (the aug five is E$\flat$—the minor third of C)
G9	same as dom7, emphasize ninth, sometimes a "one" chord (funk or blues)
G13	same as dom7, emphasize thirteenth, sometimes a "one" chord (funk or blues)
G7($\sharp$11)	same as dom7, emphasize sharp eleven and use regular fifth on weak beat, often seen as a tritone sub, see page 64
G9($\sharp$11)	same as dom7, emphasize sharp eleven and use regular fifth on weak beat
G13($\sharp$11)	same as dom7, emphasize sharp eleven and use regular fifth on weak beat
G13($\flat$9)	same as thirteenth, emphasize flat nine
G7($\flat$13)	same as G+7
G7alt.	means flat and sharp fives and nines, treat as "five" of C minor (see page 51)
G7($\sharp$9)	implies altered
G7($\sharp$9$\sharp$5)	implies altered

Other

G°7	is usually used as a passing chord (following chord is usually half step above or below) best treated as the 3, 5, $\flat$7, and $\flat$9 of a dom7($\flat$9) in this case E$\flat$7($\flat$9)
Gsus2	implies three notes G, A, and D, not usually seen in "linear" type bass parts
Gsus4	implies three notes G, C, and D, also not usually seen in "linear" type bass parts
G7sus	is created by either a full Dm7 chord with a G in the bass, or, since the relative major of D minor is F major: an Fmaj7 chord with a G in the bass. It's used as a "one" or "five" chord. Play the root at the beginning of the measure and use the rest of the measure to play the other chord's sound.
G11	same as G7sus
Gsus($\flat$9)	same as G7sus, emphasize flat nine

Putting It All Together

Almost all the lines we've worked on so far have been confined to half steps and whole steps. As you develop the ability to play these smooth lines, you become more aware of all the possibilities under your hands. While smooth sounding lines are the most challenging, they're only part of the vocabulary you need to use in musical situations. The ability to contrast smooth lines with intervals and arpeggios should be your eventual goal. Creating contrast using other elements should be part of your vocabulary as well.

Rhythm, contour, register, and harmony are the main elements that should be part of your vocabulary. Here's how they can be contrasted:

Rhythm: repetition (quarter notes) vs. rhythms (breaking it up)

Different parts of a tune might require a consistent, steady pulse or an off balance, more rhythmically broken up approach. Although the focus of this book is on the fingerboard, your number one goal should be to make the music feel good. The more subconscious your sense of harmony becomes (playing without thinking about it), the easier it is to concentrate on the overall feel of the music.

Contour: angular vs. smooth

The shape of a line can be seen best when it's written out. Smooth lines look that way on paper but occasionally they need to be broken up by more jagged sounding intervals and arpeggios.

Register: low vs. high

Staying low and "out of the way" is important, but it can be contrasted with lines that continue ascending or descending and give the music direction and momentum.

Harmony: roots and fifths vs. more chord tones and extensions

Using the basic roots and fifths is important for some situations but eventually can become predictable. Chord tones and extensions create tension and contrast.

Any or all of these elements may be necessary to use within a performance. Eventually you'll develop an instinct for providing the right amount of contrast at the right time.

Here's a bass line from a jazz CD I recorded on. Measures 1-24 and 25-48 on the next two pages are the last two times through the progression at the end of a solo. I've taken the solo out and replaced the piano with simple chords so you can hear what's going on. Except for the B♭7, it's all major seven sharp eleven or major seventh chords so there's not really a key center tying all the chords together. Each chord requires your hand to look at the key center it implies, major seven sharp eleven is a 4 chord and major seventh is a "one" chord.

Rhythm: Since I kept to pretty much all quarter notes for the first three choruses, I broke up the rhythm in the last chorus (starting measure 26) with the theme of descending from the A down to the F# starting in measure 27. This descending idea is used in different ways to break up the rhythm until measure 35 where it goes back to quarter notes. The rhythms in measures 26-34 help create tension and interest so a return to the quarter note pulse in measure 35 provides a release and also a sense of a plateau that's been reached in the music.

Contour: The variations in contours are fairly easy to see in these two choruses. The angular intervals in measure 2-4 and 6-7 are contrasted with the smooth lines in measures 9-15. Measures 17-24 are angular (hey it's hard to play smooth lines with those changes) and are contrasted with smooth lines in measures 29-39 and then more angular lines in measure 37 to the end.

Register: The contrast in register for these two choruses is not as big a feature of the bass line as the other elements. While going as low as the D♭ in measure 39, I only played as high as the B in measure 48. Within that less that two octave range you can still get a sense of motion (up and down) and direction.

Harmony: Since I played more basic roots and chord tones in the first two choruses I put more chord tones and extensions in the last two. Less than half of the last forty-eight measures have a root on beat one. Implied chords are also used in this bass line. (mentioned on pages 63 and 64). A 3-6-2-6 progression is implied to give a sense of motion to measures 7 and 8. The "five" of D major is implied on the last two beats of measure 42 and the "five" of C major is implied on the last 2 beats of measure 44.

Another thing that makes this kind of bass line work is the sense of a theme or idea being repeated. Here's where they happen:

3-6: The shape established in measure 3 is repeated in measure 4 and in measure 5 and then connected to an ascending line in measure 6.

12-16: The idea of three chromatic ascending notes starting in measure 12 is repeated exactly in measure 13 (even though the chord changes), then from different notes in measure 14, and becomes a four note ascending chromatic idea on beat 4 of measure 14 and is repeated starting on beat 2 of measure 16 to reach the E at the beginning of measure 17.

17-21: The shape in measure 17 is imitated in each measure until it changes in measure 21.

27-35: Descending idea already mentioned.

45-47: Holding the note on beat 4 and not changing until beat 2 is repeated.

One thing to remember is you eventually want all these elements to work for you as subconsciously as a language. In a performance situation if you find yourself thinking consciously about harmony or rhythm or anything else too much, then the music is probably already suffering because of it. Hopefully, by using the ideas presented in this book, you'll be able to organize harmony on the neck in a way that will allow you to make music less with your head and more instinctively like a language should be.

Good luck!

Visit Hal Leonard Online at **www.halleonard.com**

Explore the entire family of Hal Leonard products and resources